THE MODERN NATIONS IN
HISTORICAL   PERSPECTIVE

ROBIN W. WINKS, *General Editor*

The volumes in this series deal with individual
nations or groups of closely related nations
throughout the world, summarizing the chief historical trends and influences that have contributed
to each nation's present-day character, problems,
and behavior. Recent data are incorporated with
established historical background to achieve a
fresh synthesis and original interpretation.

DAVID A. G. WADDELL, the author of this volume,
is Senior Lecturer in History at the University of
Edinburgh. From 1954 to 1959 he was Lecturer
in History at the University College of the West
Indies in Jamaica, and he spent 1964-65 on se-
condment to the University of the West Indies in
Trinidad. His publications include *British Honduras: A Historical and Contemporary Survey*
(London, 1961) and various articles on the history
of the Caribbean area and other topics.

ALSO IN THE NEW WORLD SUBSERIES

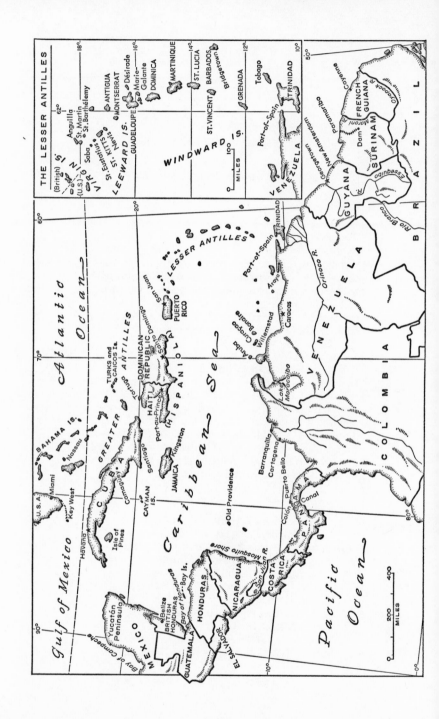

THE WEST INDIES
& THE GUIANAS

D. A. G. WADDELL

Prentice-Hall, Inc.

Englewood Cliffs, New Jersey

For
Barbara

For well over three centuries now the West Indies have been the cockpit of New World history. The first territories to be discovered, many of the islands were also the last to move toward independence. Their history is inextricably linked to three world centers, Europe, the United States, and Latin America, and for much of their history they have, therefore, been the object of plunder, conquest, and rebellion. Most of the islands were acquired by European powers long before the scramble for colonies, and the history of the West Indies is less a part of the story of imperialism than of the broad expansion of the European idea and of the European mentality. In many ways the islands stand apart from the rest of Latin America because of the colonial ties that have continued deep into the twentieth century, and not surprisingly West Indians often think of themselves within a British, French, or Dutch context rather than within the geographical context which outsiders seek to impose upon them. Thus, in a real sense, much of the history of the West Indies is a fragment of the larger European record.

But the West Indian islands also have a significant history of their own, a history which must be viewed from within in terms of the peoples of those islands rather than in relation to Europe. West Indian culture is, after all, both various and viable, and in song, story, dance, art and artifact the West Indians have contributed much to the world's cultural reservoir. Increasingly as one nears the present, the West Indian record is to be told from within the islands themselves, or in terms of developing relationships with nations other than those which first imposed their wills upon the region, relations with the United States, with Canada, and with the mainland Central American republics.

The present volume focuses upon those territories which are just emerging into a full state of independence today. Another volume in this series, John Fagg's *Cuba, Haiti and the Dominican Republic*, deals with those island-states that achieved independence at an earlier time, when policies, goals, and problems were rather different in quality if not in kind from those of today. A third book, Mario Rodríguez's *Central America*, discusses those mainland states that became independent in the preceding century, together with Panama, and a fourth volume, on Mexico, by Robert Quirk, is projected. Read together, these four books should provide a substantial picture of that economically and politically strategic area that lies between the United States and the South American continent.

Many of the West Indian territories are also members of the broader British international community today, and David Waddell's book is therefore well suited to yet another context: the study of Commonwealth History. Jamaica, Trinidad and Tobago, Guyana, and Barbados are fully independent nations within the Commonwealth, and many other island groups are dependent parts of it. The present account thus joins other published volumes in the series on Australia, New Zealand, India, Ceylon, Ghana, and Nigeria, to form—together with forthcoming works on Canada, Sierra Leone, South Africa, Central Africa, East Africa, Pakistan, and Malaysia—a comprehensive picture of how the Commonwealth of Nations emerged from the former British Empire.

Robin W. Winks
Series Editor

This book is an essay in the regional approach to West Indian history. In the past, the history of the Caribbean area was written mainly from the point of view of the imperial history of the various colonizing powers. In recent years, however, West Indian history has come to be studied and taught as an integral part of the West Indian educative process, and many of the professional historians who have emerged in the area itself have taken the view that a more meaningful interpretation of the West Indian past can be presented by treating the whole region as a unit for historical investigation. Following this trend, I have tried to analyze the general historical factors that have influenced the area as a whole and to compare their impact on different places, rather than to give a systematic account of individual territories or of the possessions of each of the imperial powers. But because of my interest in the Commonwealth, the British territories have been given somewhat fuller treatment where this has been possible within the regional conception of the study. While at some points I have made use of my own researches in original sources, I have relied mainly on the considerable and growing body of secondary authorities. Most of these, however, are concerned with particular islands or the colonies of a single power, and such originality as this study may claim lies in my attempts at synthesis and comparison. No attempt has been made to document fact or opinion, in what is conceived as an introductory essay in interpretation rather than a definitive narrative of events.

The area covered in this study consists of all those territories in the West Indian region that remained colonies until the second half of the twentieth century. This category embraces most of the islands of the Caribbean and the mainland territories of the Guianas (British, French, and Dutch) and British Honduras. The islands comprise the independent nations of Jamaica, Barbados, and Trinidad and Tobago; the American territories of Puerto Rico and the Virgin Islands; the British colonies of the Bahamas, the Cayman Islands, the Turks and Caicos Islands, the British Virgin Islands, and the seven territories in the Windward and Leeward Island groups; the French departments of Martinique and Guadeloupe; and the Netherlands Antilles. Not included are the two largest islands, Cuba and Hispaniola (comprising Haiti and the Dominican Republic), to which another volume of this Series is devoted. This division of territories with close historical and geographical affinities naturally brings with it some disadvantages, especially in dealing with the earlier centuries of West Indian history. On the other hand, the exclusion of Cuba, Haiti, and the Dominican Republic (which have been formally independent all this century) makes possible a more unified treatment of the recent past, to which the series is particularly oriented, by confining attention to those territories whose common twentieth-century experience has been of continued colonial dependence on external metropolitan powers.

In conformity with the practice in this series, the book starts with the present, my assessment of which is based largely on my own impressions, formed in the course of residence and travel in the area. Chapter One is an analytical survey of the present social, economic, and political situation in the West Indies. Chapters Three and Five are similar studies for two periods in the past: the first from the late seventeenth to the early nineteenth century, when the dominating feature over most of the area was a colonial sugar industry based on slave labor; and the second, the period in the nineteenth and early twentieth centuries characterized by the stagnation which lasted from the ending of slavery to the rise of effective nationalist movements. Chapter Two gives a brief outline of the history of the area before the "sugar revolution"; Chapter Four links the two main historical periods with an account of the transition of the islands from much-prized slave colonies to much-despised emancipated ones; and Chapter Six describes the rapid changes from the 1930s to the present.

D. A. G. W.

Contents

ONE

THE WEST INDIES TODAY

Diversity is perhaps the most obviously striking characteristic of the contemporary West Indies. Different languages are
spoken in different islands, different religions are practiced, different systems of education and social custom prevail. The physical
characteristics of the islands vary, as do the man-made elements of
the environment—the pattern of land utilization, the architecture,
the layout of town and village, the appearance and attitude of the inhabitants—so that the atmosphere of Willemstad is as unmistakably
Dutch as that of Bridgetown is English. Such distinctions continue
to be reinforced, for links with different metropolitan countries are
preserved, in ideas, in personnel, in capital, perhaps most obviously
in trade and communications, with KLM flying to Curaçao, BOAC to
Barbados, and Air France to Martinique. All this is no doubt fasci-
nating to the tourist or sociologist. But to the concerned statesman
or businessman, however much he may try to make a virtue of necessity by praising the variety of cultural riches, it can hardly be other
than vexatious. For the average person, this diversity must be simply
bewildering and a deterrent to understanding. A region containing
no more than around 8 million people and 200,000 square miles is
insignificant enough in world terms. When it consists of more than
twenty separate territories, each with its own distinctive flavor, its
physical and geographical setting, its individual historical development, all of which are important keys to the explanation of its
present state, the trouble of studying the area may seem for many
disproportionate to its importance.

It is, however, arguable that the West Indies hold a significance
for the world greater than their size and population would indicate,
and that, despite their excessive political fragmentation, the different territories share much in common both in the present and in
their historical experiences. In some respects it is possible to con-

sider the variations as superficial and the common factors as running deeper, for the problems which today face the different parts of the area are basically the same, and, for the most part, are rooted in a similar history. Socially, the whole area is experiencing to a greater or lesser degree the consequences of population explosion, diverse racial composition, and a level of welfare services low by comparison with the metropolitan countries with which it has been linked. Economically, the region, in close contact with advanced countries through trade, migration, and tourism, is sharing to the full in the "revolution of rising expectations," and finding these difficult to satisfy from an economy traditionally geared to selective external exploitation rather than balanced development. Politically, parts of the area have just emerged, and others are still emerging, from colonial relationships with metropolitan powers, under the urge of anti-colonial nationalism.

If the essential unity of the area is reflected in these common problems of the present, which are the legacies of a common past, its essential diversity is reflected in the differing solutions suggested by diverse traditions. The most obvious example of this has been the problem of metropolitan relationships, where the solutions have ranged from complete independence to complete integration. There are exceptions to almost every generalization one might try to make about the West Indies, and there are parallels in other territories for almost every individual development in any particular territory. Both unity and diversity are vital characteristics of the Caribbean past and present.

The Society

Of the total area of the administrative entities covered by this study some 90 per cent is accounted for by the mainland territories of the Guianas and British Honduras. These, however, contain only about one eighth of the total population, and have low densities of under ten people to the square mile. The islands, on the other hand, are small in land area, but are very densely populated, in most cases with more than 300 persons per square mile. This contrast is more apparent than real, for much of the land in the mainland territories is undeveloped and inaccessible, and the great bulk of the population of the Guianas is concentrated in the coastal areas, which show densities almost as high as those of the islands. Mainland and island territories alike are experiencing overpopulation in relation to their immediately exploitable resources, and the problem is becoming ever more serious with the acceleration, which has almost everywhere occurred since World War II, in the rate of natural increase of population, now in most cases exceeding 2.5 per cent per annum, and in several territories over 3 per cent.

THE PEOPLE AND THEIR ORIGINS

The prime factor in the West Indian population explosion has been the rapid fall in death rates in recent years. These are now everywhere below 15 per thousand and in many territories, including the larger ones, are below 10 per thousand. Birth rates, on the other hand, remain high, generally over 30 per thousand, and in many parts of the region over 40 per thousand. In the 1950s the absolute population growth in some territories was substantially restricted by heavy external migration, but this is now a much less significant factor. Demographic pressure in the West Indies is thus intense. It has often been argued that increased urbanization, which has been the predominant characteristic of internal West Indian migration in recent years, and rising living standards should lead to reductions in the birth rate, as happened in Western Europe and North America. But the transition from slow population increase in a period of high death and high birth rates to slow increase in a period of low death rates and low birth rates took over a century in Western Europe, during which population increased greatly as death rates were falling faster than birth rates. In the Caribbean countries the death rate has fallen much more rapidly than it did in Europe. In the 1920s and 1930s in Jamaica and Trinidad, and more recently in Puerto Rico, the falling death rates were accompanied by some decline in birth rates. But fertility in the two British islands swung up again after World War II, possibly due in part to improved health and nutrition, and no very rapid fall in birth rates can be predicted with any confidence. Even if attitudes to fertility begin to change— and some governments are now starting to sponsor population control measures—the Caribbean can probably look forward to at least another generation of substantial natural increase. The Caribbean is not, of course, the only area experiencing population explosion, but the West Indian islands, with their small areas and limited resources, do differ from larger countries in that it seems much more unlikely that the problem can be solved by means of redeployment of labor, modernization of society, and the creation of self-sufficient national economies. In most of the West Indian territories strenuous efforts have been made over the last decade to create more jobs, but the possibilities appear limited, and often the results expected seem scarcely to justify the capital expenditure required. It is not improbable that the structure of the West Indian societies may break under the strain of population pressure unless rapid external aid is forthcoming in the form of outlets for surplus population, massive capital expenditure to generate employment quickly, and preferential help in the overseas marketing of existing and new West Indian products. Only in Puerto Rico do these conditions seem adequately satisfied.

✶The diverse racial composition of the West Indies is one of the area's most notable characteristics. In a few places, some descendants of the indigenous Amerindian inhabitants of pre-Columbian times remain, but in most of the islands all traces of them have disappeared. Communities of a few thousand Amerindians still exist in the mainland territories, and of a few hundred in some of the islands, and suggestions of Amerindian admixture in the past remain in the physical appearance of some of the European population of Puerto Rico. But the present population composition of the West Indies is predominantly the result of successive waves of immigration from Europe, Africa, and Asia from the sixteenth century to the twentieth.

In the region as a whole, and in most of its component territories, the African strain is predominant. Persons classified for census purposes as of African origin preponderate in French Guiana and in all of the insular territories, except Puerto Rico, Trinidad, and a few very small islands. Most of these territories were developed in the seventeenth and eighteenth centuries by European colonists in plantations based on African slave labor. In these islands the next most important racial grouping is Afro-European (in some places referred to as "colored" or "brown"), and there are small minorities of Europeans, and in some places of Asiatics and Amerindians. In Jamaica, the most populous of this group, Africans account for 76 per cent of the population, Afro-Europeans for 15 per cent, Europeans for less than 1 per cent, with slightly under 5 per cent made up about equally of Asiatics and Afro-Asiatics. In some of the other islands the African percentage is larger and the Afro-European smaller, while in others the reverse is true. But in all, the combined African and Afro-European populations (a grouping sometimes referred to as "creole") reach around 90 per cent, and in none does the European exceed about 5 per cent.

In Trinidad, Guyana, and Surinam, in addition to African and Afro-European elements, there are substantial Asiatic segments in the population, introduced mainly as indentured plantation laborers in the nineteenth and early twentieth centuries. East Indians account for 36 per cent of the population in Trinidad, 48 per cent in Guyana, and 35 per cent in Surinam, where a further 17 per cent of Indonesian origin swell the Asiatic proportion. Africans form 43 per cent of Trinidad's population and 33 per cent of Guyana's, and in Surinam the Creole community, consisting of Africans and Afro-Europeans, amounts to 44 per cent. This last figure does not include some 30,000 people of African origin, descendants of escaped slaves known as the Bush Negroes, who follow a primitive life in the interior, and are not integrated into Surinam society. They are not included in the census figures, and their estimated numbers would represent an addition of some 10-15 per cent to the total population of the territory. In British Honduras, Africans and Afro-Europeans account for over half of the population, but there is a significant Amerindian and *mestizo*, or Euro-Amerindian, minority, descended from immigrants from the adjacent Latin American territories and amounting to some 30 per cent of the population. Puerto Rico, which did not develop into a plantation colony until after the African slave trade had been abolished, is the major exception to the pattern of non-European predominance, its population being classified as approximately 80 per cent "white" and 20 per cent "nonwhite," a category including both Africans and Afro-Europeans.

An interesting feature of the ethnic composition of the area is the contrast between the high degree of racial integration between African and European, as evidenced by the large Afro-European segments in many territories, and the low degree of integration of the more recently arrived Asiatics, who have not intermarried much with either Africans or Europeans. The significance of such a distinction for the societies of the region is, however, rather a disputed question. While it is possible to draw a contrast between the "plural" societies with large East Indian elements and the unitary societies where this element is not present, it has been argued, on the one hand, that the factors separating African from non-African in Jamaica are such as to justify terming it a "plural" society, and, on the other, that the coexistence between Africans and East Indians in Guyana renders it a single society.

Much of the area was first exploited by European enterprise and African slave labor for the raising of tropical agricultural commodities for European markets. Of these the most important was sugar, and this remains a vital crop on many islands. The area is still primarily engaged in agriculture and sugar is still the main crop, but the contribution of agriculture to the national income has declined, as has the percentage of the labor force engaged in agricultural work. Since the ending of slavery the social dominance of the plantation has diminished in several territories, and the significance of the small peasant farmer has increased. Agricultural labor on plantations has traditionally carried with it the stigma of slavery and, in some territories, subsequent indenture, and is an occupation of low prestige and, normally, of little skill. In most islands peasant farming is suffering from population pressure, and there is a consequential population drift to the towns and to non-agricultural pursuits, and also, where possible, overseas migration. In the twentieth century other occupations have emerged with the development of large-scale oil refining in the Netherlands Antilles and Trinidad, bauxite mining in the Guianas and Jamaica, and manufacturing industries and tourism, especially in Puerto Rico and Jamaica. Another traditional avenue of employment has been domestic service, but this is declining with the rise of opportunities in commercialized service occupations.

Until very recently there has been, and still is in several places, a great gulf between unskilled agricultural, general laboring, and domestic occupations, carrying low income and status and usually almost exclusively filled by persons of African or East Indian origin, and a small élite of employers, landowners, public servants, and professional men, mainly European (and often expatriate) or Afro-European of light complexion. A middle class has now emerged in most places, with the expansion of business and public services, and occupational mobility is increasing. However, except perhaps in Puerto Rico, a strong bias persists toward traditionally high status occupations such as professional or even clerical work, rather than business and technical occupations, in which many of the expanding opportunities lie.

SOCIAL STRUCTURE AND STANDARDS

Social stratification is highly complex, being based on considerations of birth, wealth, and occupation. Parentage is readily identifiable through skin pigmentation and other physical racial characteristics, and is probably still the most significant index of status. In most cases it remains true that the lighter the skin, the more European and less African the appearance, the higher the social status. It is still common for dark-skinned social aspirants to marry wives lighter than themselves and so "improve the color" of the family. The relative social disability of African appearance can, however, be offset to some extent by wealth—which, to be effective for this purpose, must be conspicuously displayed—and by high status occupations, such as the professions. In the absence of rigid color bars, and with the expansion of educational and occupational opportunities, upward mobility for those of non-European origin has been much facilitated.

Until very recently, a rise in the social scale in most places involved not only compensation in wealth or occupation for "adverse" racial attributes, but the adoption of the élite's behavior patterns, in mode of speech, consumption habits, recreations, and the like. As colonial élites were, for the most part, metropolitan oriented, successful integration was difficult to achieve and involved a degree of alienation from the majority of the society. In recent years, with the loosening of colonial ties, and the enlargement of middle sector opportunities, middle classes have begun to emerge, which are rather more locally oriented in their value systems and behavior patterns, and less alienated from the culture of the mass of the society. These sectors are the main sources of political and cultural leadership and the main focus of the working out of national identities to replace the former colonial ones. At the same time these groups are concerned with maintaining and improving their economic status, and emphasizing their social elevation over the general mass of the population. It is not surprising if their members at times appear under undue strain, and are not always unerring in judgment.

West Indian levels of living, as indicated by per capita national income figures, fall somewhere in the middle of the world range. The larger and richer territories are better off than the vast majority of underdeveloped countries, while even the smaller and poorer enjoy higher incomes than almost any country in Africa or Asia. On the other hand, the West Indies still lag a long way behind the advanced countries of Europe and North America. While the Caribbean is largely free of the abject want and starvation often encountered in Africa and Asia, poverty certainly is still widespread, and a majority of West Indians live at a level that would probably be regarded as unacceptably low in Europe or North America.

Such information as is available on nutrition suggests that many West Indians are still undernourished, and that the caloric intake of many more is barely above the minimum normally regarded as necessary for healthy existence. Throughout the region, diets tend to contain an unduly high proportion of starches, and local sources of foods of high protein content are inadequate. Indeed, a large proportion of food requirements of all kinds have to be imported into most of the territories. This stems in part from a continuation of the traditional orientation of agricultural production toward exports, in part from long-established preferences for imported foods stimulated by such a trading pattern, and in part from the inability of often uneconomically small peasant holdings to cater efficiently to the growing non-agricultural sectors. It is, however, highly probable that the incidence of malnutrition has declined considerably since World War II.

One consequence of somewhat improved nutrition is some improvement in standards of health. But here the most dramatic improvement has been shown in the fall of mortality rates to levels approximating those of Europe, largely due to the elimination of certain diseases which were formerly frequent causes of death. This, however, is only one aspect of improved health. Morbidity rates have probably not improved to anything like the same extent, and there is probably still much scope for the reduction of preventible, though non-fatal, disease, and the consequent lessening of personal suffering and impairment of productivity, through improved sanitation and medical services, which in most places are at present seriously overstrained. Nevertheless, the region cannot, on the whole, be regarded as in any sense an unhealthy one, nor can the medical services in most territories be regarded as intolerably inadequate.

It is in housing that deviations from levels acceptable in more advanced countries are most obvious. The great majority of houses are small wooden structures with galvanized metal roofs, seldom with proper cooking or toilet facilities. Frequently several of these houses share a common yard. Domestic electricity and running water, main sewerage and street lighting are uncommon. Durable household goods are usually minimal, and a high proportion of houses contain only one room. In several places the erection of modern concrete dwellings for low-income families has been encouraged or undertaken by governments. While such houses usually mean a considerable improvement over the occupants' previous accommodation, floor areas remain small and overcrowding (in the sense, for example, of parents and children sleeping in the same room) general. For each family fortunate enough to occupy such a modern home, there is probably at least one other in an unfloored makeshift structure of scrap metal and cardboard.

At the other end of the scale, the middle classes are often better housed than equivalent income groups in European countries. There has traditionally been little provision of housing for economic groups in intermediate positions between the relatively affluent middle classes and the poor mass of the population, though with the great expansion of people in this category modest though adequate homes are beginning to appear, often through government-sponsored schemes.

Until recently, communal public amenities have been much neglected, largely because of the exclusiveness of the élites and their separation from the mass of the population. Much more attention is now being paid to such matters, and the governments are encouraging or undertaking the creation or development of community centers, recreation grounds, public parks and beaches, museums, libraries, and the like. But much remains to be done both in extending such facilities and in educating the public to make constructive use of them.

EDUCATION AND CULTURE

In common with most other underdeveloped areas, the West Indies sees the improvement of the educational facilities of the mass of the population as an indispensable prerequisite for any form of social progress, and authorities throughout the area have in recent years accorded education very high priority. This is doubly necessary, for not only is more and better education required, but it is required for a rapidly expanding number of children—the result of continued high birth rates and steeply declining infant mortality rates. Until recently there has been little or no provision for the mass of the population after the age of fourteen; many children have failed to complete six years of schooling and have remained at least functionally illiterate, although illiteracy rates in general have tended to fall substantially. In most places school attendance is technically compulsory for children between the ages of six and fourteen, but there are seldom enough school places for all children in these age groups, and the laws are frequently not enforced. Secondary education, mainly in private or denominational schools, was, until recently, virtually confined to middle-class children. Though considerable expansion has taken place in secondary as well as primary schools and many more children are gaining high school qualifications, provision is still limited through scarcities of money, of qualified teachers, and of accommodation, so that competition for secondary school places remains intense.

Population pressure is the greatest problem in West Indian education, but by no means the only one. The raising of standards in primary education and the maintenance of secondary school standards in the face of enormous expansion are also questions of much concern. Equally important is the question of curricula, which have traditionally been rather academic and geared to the requirements of metropolitan examining bodies. Adaptation of content to local needs has been proceeding for some time, but there is resistance to any trend in commercial or technical directions in the educational as well as in the occupational field.

Higher education is also under great pressure. Until recently few opportunities existed except for the wealthy who sent their children abroad to universities. Although the University of Puerto Rico was set up in 1903 on the model of the state universities of the United States, its general impact was small until after World War II, when a great expansion took place both there and in some smaller private institutions. In the British West Indies a University College, affiliated with the University of London, was set up in Jamaica in 1948. The emphasis was placed on quality rather than quantity of graduates, and numbers increased slowly in its first decade. Expansion has been more rapid since about 1959; the University extended its activities to Trinidad in 1960, became the independent University of the West Indies in 1962, and in 1963 set up a new College in Barbados. British Guiana participated in the University College of the West Indies until 1963, and then set up its own institution, the University of Guyana, which has so far remained small and caters to part-time students at a lower level than the University of the West Indies. Despite the existence of a local institution, large numbers of West Indians continue to study in the United States, Canada, and the United Kingdom. The French and Dutch territories are still without local institutions at the university level. In addition to educating numbers of Caribbean students, local universities have been responsible for stimulating and undertaking much research bearing on the area. Much of the most significant work on the Caribbean in recent years has emerged from these institutions, which have also played an important role as centers for researchers from outside the region. While in general the educational problems of the region are similar, the solutions, in terms of the philosophy, content, and practice of education, have varied in accordance with metropolitan traditions.

Language is perhaps the most obvious divisive force in the area, and the most enduring legacy of imperial control. English is the official language in the British and Commonwealth territories, French in the French territories, Dutch in the Netherlands territories, and both English and Spanish in Puerto Rico. Despite more than half a century of American possession and influence, Spanish remains firmly rooted as the first language of the vast majority of Puerto Ricans. In the other territories Creole dialects of the European languages are spoken by the mass of the people. These are basically European in vocabulary, but contain much syntax and many words of African origin. Jamaican Creole differs considerably from the English dialects of the Eastern Caribbean, and in territories where French influence was important, such as Dominica, St. Lucia, Grenada, and, to a lesser extent, Trinidad, a French patois similar to that of Guadeloupe and Martinique is commonly spoken. In some of the Netherlands Antilles the local language is Papiamento, a combination of various European and African languages, and in Surinam a somewhat similar synthesis has produced another Creole language. Asiatic immigrants have preserved little of their native speech, but the Bush Negroes of Surinam and the Amerindians of Guyana and British Honduras still speak African or Amerindian languages. In the latter territory there is also a substantial Spanish-speaking minority.

Within the various territories there are often problems of communication between the élite, whose speech approximates to the received pronunciation of the metropolitan language, and the mass of the people, who deviate greatly from this. Thus speech is a significant status index. English is generally understood among élite and middle groups in the Dutch Antilles and Puerto Rico, and thus for most of the area English is a satisfactory working means of communication. But to view the territories here under discussion in isolation would be to offer a misleading linguistic picture, for most of the remainder of the Caribbean and circum-Caribbean region is Spanish-speaking, the main exception being Haiti where a Creole form of French is spoken. Linguistic diversity remains a serious obstacle to regional integration, and a greater problem than the multilingualism within certain territories. The significance of linguistic diversity is not confined to problems of communication. Language is, of course, also one of the principal repositories of a culture, and one of the principal symbols of a cultural identity. Thus the retention of Spanish is an important feature of the campaign of those Puerto Ricans who wish to resist absorption by the culture of the United States. On the other hand, the preservation of French is a necessary aspect of the metropolitan integration policy in the French territories. Local dialects in the British territories are being no longer dismissed as simply bad English, but are being investigated and nurtured as an element in local national culture, and fostered by some elements of the intelligentsia, who use them as media for literary or dramatic work and see them as valuable parts of the folk culture which merit preservation.

Religion, like language, is closely identified with the retention of cultural origins. This is particularly noticeable in the case of the East Indians of Trinidad, Guyana, and Surinam. Most of these are Hindu, but many are Moslem, as are the Surinam Javanese, and there are smaller groups of other oriental religions. In other parts of the area various primitive cults, at least partly African in origin, are preserved—in their most complete form among the Bush Negroes in Surinam, and in a more superficial form as Shango and Pocomania among relatively urbanized groups in Trinidad and Jamaica. In a slightly different category are the Ras Tafarians of Jamaica, who recognize the divinity of the Emperor of Ethiopia, which they regard as their homeland. But this is a recent development in Jamaica, not without political motivation, rather than a continuing religious tradition.

In every territory, and in the region as a whole, the great majority of the population is Christian. In Puerto Rico, in the French and most of the Dutch territories, in Trinidad, Dominica, Grenada, St. Lucia, and British Honduras, Roman Catholics form a majority, and the Roman Catholic church is a significant force in society. In Jamaica, the smaller Dutch islands, Barbados, and the remaining British islands, Protestants are in a majority. In the British islands the Church of England has most adherents, but it is possible that many are nominal, and that the most dynamic element in Protestantism is represented by a variety of fundamental evangelical sects, sometimes with links in the United States, and usually drawing their parsons as well as their followers from the lower ranks of society. In most territories religion, particularly in its more fundamentalist forms, plays an important part in the social life of the mass of the people, the churches providing opportunities for satisfying status aspirations not available in the wider society as a whole, and the observances providing important opportunities for emotional release. Where religious diversity exists, it is seldom an important divisive factor in itself, either within a territory or between neighboring territories, and is thus one of the less significant obstacles to national or regional integration. However, religion is frequently an additional factor reinforcing divisions of a racial, class, or cultural nature.

Many observers have seen the creative life of the region as divided between the derivative cultures of the metropolitan-oriented élites and the traditional folkways of the descendants of the slaves. Whereas the former have responded to the changing fashions of the metropolitan centers, the latter have long been divorced from the African part of their origins, and have become thoroughly creolized, and thus may be considered more indigenous and more autonomus. Nationalism has dictated efforts to preserve some forms of folk expression, to interest the élites in them, and on this basis to build identifiably Caribbean art forms. The best known results of this process are the calypso and the steel-band of Trinidad, both of which have suffered somewhat from the respectability accorded to recognized institutions.

The arts have as yet relatively few local patrons and have had to rely for much of their support on wider markets—particularly tourists from the United States, whose tastes appear to tend toward either the wildly exotic or the highly conventional with West Indian picturesqueness added. In view of these relatively lucrative possibilities and the general limitations of the market, it is perhaps remarkable that even limited progress has been made toward creating specifically West Indian art forms as an expression of a West Indian cultural identity.

Few creative works by West Indians have yet emerged that are both good and West Indian, although there is a great deal of literature and art which makes an effective protest at the state of the West Indies. Much of what is good is, however, only slightly West Indian, and much of what is thoroughly West Indian is inferior.

The West Indies still await writers and artists of genius to aid in their quest for identity.

The Economy

The colonial economy of the West Indies was built on the fertility of the land and the advantages of a climate characterized by abundant warmth and rainfall. Lying within the Tropic of Cancer, but influenced by the northeast trade winds, the West Indies experience temperatures that seldom drop below 60° F or rise above 95° F. Although there are some arid pockets, and other areas of extremely heavy precipitation, in most places annual rainfall is around fifty inches, with a marked seasonal incidence, the first few months of the year normally being dry, and the last few wet, with a less marked rainy season around May and dry season around August. The complicated geology of the region has produced a great diversity of soil types, many of which are rich in nutrients for a wide variety of tropical crops.

RESOURCES

Although agriculture was the foundation of West Indian historical development, and to a great extent remains the principal basis of the economies of many territories, it alone cannot be expected to maintain the large and rising populations now to be found. The total land area is small and much of it is unexploitable. In Jamaica, for example, attempted exploitation of hill areas has led to serious erosion, and the denuding of forest cover in watershed areas has led to loss of rainfall. Other islands, notably Antigua, have chronic water shortage problems. In the mainland territories, lack of communications and capital for land development have retarded the opening up of new areas of potential agricultural value. In addition to such physical problems, systems of land tenure in some areas have encouraged excessive division of holdings; lack of clear legal titles and the existence of customary family rights to land have inhibited full exploitation; social and political factors have prevented mechanization on large estates; and the use of landownership for purposes of prestige, security, or speculation has kept some valuable land unproductive. While land reform and agricultural planning have been much in the air in recent years, major development efforts have mainly been made in other directions, less politically explosive and less limited in potential.

Few of the territories have significant natural resources of other kinds to supplement their agriculture. Only Jamaica, Guyana, and Surinam, with substantial quantities of bauxite, in which they are among the world's largest producers, and Trinidad, with limited reserves of petroleum, have important mineral potentialities. Coal is not found, and only in the Guianas are water resources adequate for the large-scale generation of hydroelectric power, though Puerto Rico generates some 20 per cent of its electricity requirements by this means. Economies small in size and relatively low in purchasing power offer strictly limited markets for local manufacturing industry, and although sea communications between many of the territories are easy, the similarity of their economies gives little scope for interisland trade. In many territories the only other exploitable natural resource is the beauty of the locale which, combined with the warm climate, has given rise to a tourist industry.

The human resources of the islands are quantitatively but not qualitatively abundant. The vast majority of the labor forces are unskilled or semi-skilled, and tend to be underutilized. Unemployment rates are high, underemployment and seasonal work common. Labor is not, however, as cheap as its abundance and low skills might suggest. Labor unions have long been active in the area, and are particularly strong among certain types of unskilled occupation, where they have succeeded in raising wage rates and improving job security. Thus, even in a flooded labor market many employers would find labor-saving devices economic, but the introduction of these in established industries meets with union resistance. Facilities for technical education are generally inadequate, and the retention of skilled labor has proved difficult in view of greater opportunities offered by emigration. While there is an overall shortage of trained personnel, both at the skilled level and at managerial and professional levels, there have sometimes been short-term difficulties in finding suitable posts for highly trained West Indians, and the consequent frustrations have tended to worsen the situation. While in general the tendency is to West Indianize senior positions formerly held by expatriates from the metropolitan countries, it has not always been possible to equate the supply of with the demand for particular skills. It is probably true, as is often alleged, that in countries such as Jamaica the number of expatriates, especially in government employment, has actually risen since independence above the number in the last days of colonial rule, as a result of development schemes calling for various kinds of particular expertise not available within the community.

In capital resources, both public and private, the region is reasonably well endowed. In most places substantial fixed assets in the form of communication facilities and public utilities have long existed, and there has been much recent development, though it is probable that these services are still barely adequate to meet the strain being placed upon them by the development process. Large productive enterprises, such as sugar, bauxite, and oil, have been largely foreign-owned, and able to call on overseas sources of more liquid capital. Many of the new developments of recent years have also been financed from abroad, either by private investment, government borrowing, or foreign aid grants or "soft" loans. Capital from such sources, however, has not always been directed in accordance with the priorities called for by development plans, and it has also proved difficult to mobilize the substantial, if limited, amounts of available local capital for development purposes, by drawing it away from its traditional investment outlets—commerce and land speculation—into such fields as manufacturing and government loans.

PRODUCTION AND TRADE

In the region as a whole, and in most of the component territories, agriculture is the most important activity in terms of labor employed. In several territories it is also the most important sector in terms of national income, and in the export trade. To a large extent agricultural efforts are still, as traditionally, directed toward the production of a limited number of crops for export, and sugar remains, as it has been for centuries, by far the most important. The West Indies, however, produce only a small fraction of world sugar output, and their production is not large enough to have any great influence on world markets. Much of the sugar is produced in large estates, for the most part owned by large foreign companies, but in some territories companies are obliged to process an increasing amount of cane grown by small farmers. In view of its key position in these poor economies, the sugar industry has increasingly become a political and social, as well as an economic, enterprise. Under its present labor-intensive structure, the West Indian sugar industry could not compete in a free world sugar market. There has, however, been no such market since World War II, and the sugar industry has been maintained by an elaborate system of guaranteed prices and quotas in metropolitan markets. In the British territories, for example, the Commonwealth Sugar Agreement has been a vital prop to island economies, ensuring much employment and foreign exchange. Inasmuch as this has involved an element of subsidy from the metropolitan consumer, it has been natural for the benefits to be spread as widely as possible, in the form of employment for seasonal field laborers and cane farmers. While this policy has undoubtedly alleviated much of the hardship which the failure or contraction of the industry would have caused, it has also inhibited the measures of rationalization, modernization, and mechanization which might have made the industry competitive in the future. Although there is no immediate likelihood of an end to artificial markets in sugar, clearly this industry cannot be expected to contribute significantly to any solution to the increasing economic or demographic problems of the area.

No other export crop is as pervasive or significant as sugar, but in several territories others are of some importance. In Jamaica and the Lesser Antilles bananas are exported to European markets, and a variety of other crops figure in the export lists. Most of the growing of these is done by small farmers, while the shipping and overseas marketing are in the hands of large foreign concerns, with only a limited commitment to any particular producing area. As most tropical agricultural products are in actual or potential world oversupply, little promise of substantial development would seem to lie in more intensive exploitation of minor export crops.

More important is the production of food crops for local consumption. In most territories there is a substantial body of subsistence farmers, who dispose of such small surpluses as they may produce at local weekly markets. In general such farming, even when assisted by government marketing schemes, is inefficient, neither giving the farmer a good living, exploiting the land potential, nor supplying the needs of the consumer. In almost all territories food stands very high on the list of imports, and the substitution of locally produced for imported foodstuffs has for some time been seen as an obvious means of helping to solve such important and acute problems as the drain of foreign exchange, and the underuse of land and labor. Implementation of such a policy has, however, been very difficult. Consumers have well established preferences for imported foods, often better (or at least more standardized) in quality, and lower in price, despite freight and import charges, than local products. Undoubtedly more food could be produced within the islands, particularly meat and dairy products, which are heavily imported; but it seems unlikely that satisfactory supplies could be raised without changes in land tenure, and in production and marketing organization. Here again economic desirability conflicts with the political necessity of placating the voting small holder or peasant proprietor.

Mineral production is of considerable importance in Jamaica, Guyana, Surinam, and Trinidad, but there is little or none in the other territories. The Caribbean is one of the world's leading producing areas of bauxite, which accounts for some half of the value of the exports of Jamaica, around one third of those of Guyana, and over two thirds of those of Surinam. Reserves in all three territories appear to be considerable, and there are good prospects of this product continuing to be an important support to these economies for many years to come. Operations are, however, dependent on the state of the world aluminum market, and West Indian production is controlled by subsidiaries of North American aluminum manufacturers. Parent companies have been rather slow to undertake processing locally, most preferring to ship the bauxite raw, but some bauxite is now being locally converted into alumina in all three territories, and in Surinam local processing is going further, for a smelter is under construction, in conjunction with a hydroelectric scheme, for the conversion of alumina to aluminum. The possibilities of similar development in Guyana have not been fully explored but would seem comparable with those in Surinam. Jamaica, however, lacks the hydroelectric potential for aluminum production under present processes. While the impact of an aluminum industry on the area is still a question for the future, the benefits of local conversion to alumina are already clearly demonstrable. It has been calculated that Jamaica derives three times as much benefit, in local expenditures and revenue, from a ton of bauxite converted into alumina before export, as from a ton of bauxite shipped raw. Thus, if all bauxite mined were converted into alumina, Jamaica could receive the same economic benefits for a much smaller loss of mineral reserves, or could receive much larger benefits for the same bauxite consumption. It seems likely that there will be increasing pressure on the producers to carry out more and more of their processing locally. As bauxite mining is not labor intensive, the main advantages lie in finance rather than in employment. At the same time, local labor has benefited substantially from periods of construction work, and, in Jamaica at least, agricultural practices and local food production have been improved by the farming operations of the bauxite companies in land either held for future operations, or rehabilitated after working out.

Petroleum is produced in Trinidad on a scale sufficient to be important to the local economy, but scarcely significant in terms of world production. The geological formation of the island makes for high-cost production, and known reserves are not great. Much more important to Trinidad than oil drilling is the oil processing industry. The island boasts two refineries, one of which is very large and capable of producing a wide range of specialized petroleum products. These process much imported crude oil, as well as Trinidad's own production. Petroleum products are the predominant item in Trinidad's international trade, and the oil industry provides much of the Trinidad government's revenue. Oil refining is also the principal industry of the Dutch islands of Curaçao and Aruba, each of which has a very large refinery processing crude oil from the neighboring Venezuelan oilfields. In recent years, however, Venezuelan policy has obliged oil companies to refine much more of their crude produce within Venezuelan territory, and production in the Dutch islands has had to be cut back. No other minerals are of great economic significance, although manganese in Guyana and gypsum in Jamaica are produced on an exportable scale.

Except in the form of the processing of some local raw materials, especially sugar cane, manufactures played no part in colonial economies, requirements being supplied by metropolitan countries. Only since World War II has manufacturing begun to assume importance. Most recently established manufacturing industries have been of light consumer goods, substituting for items previously imported. As the local markets are very small, products have often been of poorer quality and higher price than the imported article, against which protective measures have had to be taken. Because industrialization has been seen as a major potential contributor to the process of economic growth generally, and to the problem of alleviating unemployment in particular, most governments have been prepared to give industries not only tariff protection, but positive inducements such as tax holidays, in the hope of attracting investment in this field. Concern for the effects on the balance of payments of the high levels of imported manufactures has also been a factor favoring the stimulation of local industries, but its importance is of course limited by the fact that many, perhaps most, of the raw materials for industrial production have to be imported. Exports of manufactures are relatively limited, except in cases where the industry has been set up specifically for export purposes, often as a subsidiary of a parent company in the importing country. This has been particularly common in Puerto Rico, where many firms have taken advantage of lower wage and tax rates to produce for the United States market. Even if all materials are imported and all products exported, such enterprises benefit the island economies to the extent that the value of the labor is exported. Puerto Rico, with the valuable advantage of free access to the United States market, already has established a considerable industrial sector. In Jamaica and Trinidad manufactures are assuming an increasingly important role in the economies, but in most territories they are still of small importance.

Undoubtedly the greatest obstacle in the way of industrial development is the smallness of the home markets. Even a regional West Indian economy would afford rather too small a market for many types of industry, and any high degree of economic coordination seems unlikely in the immediate future. Difficulties over the implications of regional economic planning were indeed a factor in the disruption of the short-lived federation of the British West Indian territories. Further problems in the way of rapid industrialization are shortages of skills both at managerial and operative level, and a suspicion of foreign investment capital, combined with a reluctance of local capital to forsake its traditional outlets for somewhat speculative enterprises.

Economic growth, population explosion, and rising expectations in the field of social services have combined to bring about a large increase in the numbers employed in public service occupations, while changing social attitudes have led to a lessening of the importance of domestic service as a field of employment, and a rise in commercial personal services, catering to an expanding middle class. Construction everywhere is an important sector of the economy, and a large-scale employer of labor, and inasmuch as this is devoted to the improvement of the infrastructure in such fields as communications, or to the improvement of human resources through educational and health services, it should contribute to the subsequent expansion of other sectors. The smaller territories, however, appear to carry overelaborate governmental structures, and, in the realm of specialized services, have the choice of providing none, or having them underutilized.

One service industry, tourism, is of vital importance to the economy of many territories, and a valuable source of invisible exports. Indeed, tourism is probably the most dominant element in the international image of the Caribbean area. The West Indies have benefited from the world boom in tourism, particularly of Americans, in the last decade, and have taken some steps to adapt themselves from a preserve of the very rich to the requirements of a mass tourist trade. Puerto Rico is easily the most visited territory, followed by Jamaica; in the Eastern Caribbean tourism is well established in the American Virgin Islands, Barbados, and Antigua, and most other territories are trying to cash in on the traffic, often with active government support. Despite its importance as a dollar earner, the tourist industry is not without its local critics, who argue that, because of the part fashion plays in tourist habits, it is an unsound basis for an economy; that it diverts investment and training programs from more solid forms of activity; and, above all, that it demoralizes a small country by subordinating its cultural tastes to those of its visitors and by producing a servile, tip-begging attitude in its populace. This last is felt to be particularly serious in communities still seeking their national identities, and hampered by a legacy of slavery and racial prejudice. While the visitor is likely to encounter ample evidence of instances of such demoralization, he has much to offer the area in employment opportunities, and the Caribbean has much to offer him in climate and natural beauty. In these circumstances the tourist industry seems likely to grow rather than to decline.

Despite the developments and diversifications of recent years, the colonial patterns of the economies of the region persist to a very great extent. This is reflected in their trading patterns: in the significance of foreign trade in the economy, in the products involved in foreign trade, and in the foreign trading partners. In several places over half of the domestic product is exported, and the import trade generally exceeds the export in value. Exports are principally agricultural and mineral products, except in Puerto Rico where the manufactured products of light industries are already of greater importance. In most territories a few commodities dominate the export trade. Much of the food requirements of the area continue to be imported, as do most manufactured consumer goods. In recent years, however, the process of economic development has led to increased imports of capital goods and raw materials for new industries.

In almost all cases the bulk of overseas trade is with the metropolitan or former metropolitan countries. In the case of Puerto Rico, Martinique, Guadeloupe, Barbados, and the British Windward and Leeward Islands, the preponderance of exports and imports are exchanged with the United States, France, and Britain, respectively. In the bauxite producing countries a substantial proportion of exports go to North America, while Trinidad and the Dutch Antilles import large quantities of crude oil from Venezuela and elsewhere, and export oil products to a variety of consumers. Throughout the area the United States is an important source of imports, and in the case of the Commonwealth territories, Canadian trade is of some significance. While these patterns derive largely from the past, and are facilitated by long-established trade connections and communications, they are reinforced and perpetuated by tariff or quota preferences given by the metropolitan countries to their associated territories, and corresponding preferences accorded by the Caribbean countries to goods from their own metropolis.

Most Caribbean countries have in recent years shown substantial trading deficits. The balance of payments has normally been reconciled by overseas capital investment, foreign aid and loans, and tourist expenditure. In a sense this situation can be regarded as a natural concomitant of economic development, and many of the imports may contribute to the future solution of balance of payments problems. The deficits do, however, explain the general preoccupation with greater self-sufficiency in food production and with attempts to manufacture import substitutes. Increased prosperity in the region has inevitably been reflected in an increased demand for imported goods, often of a luxury nature, and in some territories controls have been applied in an attempt to restrain the "import explosion." In addition to the obvious physical or marketing limitations of export expansion, a further factor has been the tendency in recent years for the terms of trade to move against the West Indies, as against primary producing areas generally.

ECONOMIC DEVELOPMENT

Economic development has been seen as an urgent necessity in the West Indies, and has been accorded high priority in both metropolitan and local policies. Demographic pressures alone would demand expansion in the economies, which their traditional patterns would seem scarcely capable of making. But perhaps even more acute are the pressures of rising material expectations. West Indians are probably better aware than the people of any other developing area of how the wealthier half of the world lives, and of the currents of world opinion toward greater social justice, more equal opportunities, and the mitigation of poverty. Living in small, literate communities, closely connected with North America and Europe through migration, trade, and tourism, they are, with the exception of relatively few isolated pockets, well in the stream of world affairs. The problem of living standards has been brought closer to home by the recent rapid rise to affluence of the expanding local middle classes.

The very urgency of these problems has, however, affected the approach to development, by posing difficult choices between short- and long-term measures, and in general the short-term measures have found favor. As a result some remarkable growth rates have been attained, and in general throughout the region real national income per capita has tended to rise, and an increasing aura of apparent prosperity is noticeable. On the other hand, there has been relatively little change in the structure of the economies, and it is somewhat doubtful whether any territory has moved appreciably nearer a position of self-sustained growth. Moreover, increases in per capita national incomes tend to obscure the significance of continued high unemployment rates, of great inequalities in the distribution of income and wealth, and of the propensity of the affluent to consume imported goods rather than to invest in the local economy.

Though lip-service has been paid to the idea of development and economic planning, which has been widely regarded as a panacea for all the region's ills, governments have tended to approach development as a means of meeting immediate political necessities, rather than as a means of trying to ensure a viable future for the country. Development and planning have been territorial rather than regional, despite the fact that in the long-term it is not easy to see a very promising future for any individual unit. The area has seen little evidence of constructive economic thinking along the lines of what sort of attainable economy might give a territory an acceptable level of living by the end of the century, and what steps would have to be taken immediately if there were to be any chance of bringing it about.

Some reasons may be suggested for this relatively short-sighted view of the future. One is that many of the imponderables involved in looking more than a few years ahead are susceptible to only the most minimal control from economies so largely dependent on the outside world. In these circumstances the most far-sighted plans could be rendered valueless by an unkind twist of a remote fate, or rendered unnecessary by an unexpected gift from the gods; thus both optimists and pessimists see little point in constructive thinking. A second explanation is that rational projections of trends which are at present virtually inescapable in most territories are likely to produce a medium-term prospect so depressing as to be well-nigh unthinkable. On this view, it is understandable to plan development in a short-term context, and, beyond that to hope for the best, while fearing the worst. Finally, and most important, the depth of the region's commitment to economic development may be questioned. There have been only very limited attempts to integrate the objectives of economic development with other social goals. There has been little sign of any widespread and determined tendency to subordinate immediate gratification to a highly hypothetical better future, or to sacrifice cherished social customs and modes of thought on the altar of imported concepts of progress.

Politics

The territories of the region have recently experienced common political urges to move away from colonial status. But, with power and jurisdiction lying in the hands of metropolitan governments, local demands have had to be largely formulated in accordance with metropolitan ideas of political advance. These have varied from power to power, and have been modified by changing world opinions of the criteria for independence, and the possible forms of political relationship. Many West Indian territories have satisfied some of the traditional criteria of nationhood, such as internal unity, cultural homogeneity, literacy, and political sophistication, but have failed to satisfy others, because of smallness of area, population, and resources, racial heterogeneity, poverty, and economic dependence. The problem of smallness might have been rendered less important through regional amalgamation, but, while there has been much talk of this on the economic level, neither local nor metropolitan authorities have shown much interest in regional political cooperation. The political context has been, at widest, that of the possessions of a single power, and more normally, especially in local eyes, that of the individual island. In these circumstances a variety of political forms and a variety of types of relationship with the metropolis have emerged in the region. The solutions adopted have by no means solved all the problems, nor have they proved completely satisfactory either to the West Indies or to the metropolitan powers.

METROPOLITAN RELATIONSHIPS

Complete independence might seem the most clear-cut political solution to the problem of ending colonial status. Yet only four territories, all British—Jamaica, Trinidad and Tobago, Guyana, and Barbados—reached it by 1966. This was a rather obvious goal for British possessions, as it had been the declared objective of British colonial policy even before World War II, and as ample precedents were available, within a few years of the ending of the war, of former British possessions attaining independence and retaining, if they chose, a link with Britain through membership in the Commonwealth. From the West Indian point of view, the problem was not so much that of Britain's ultimate intentions, as that of her criteria, for Britain appeared to demand a certain size and degree of economic viability as a prerequisite for independence, and seemed at first prepared to recognize only a federation of the British West Indian territories as meeting this requirement. However, by the late 1950s it became clear that at least some territories could be regarded as able to qualify for independence on their own, and when the West Indies federation broke up, Jamaica and Trinidad and Tobago went their separate ways to become independent members of the Commonwealth in 1962. Guyana, its progress delayed by internal political divisions, followed in 1966, as did Barbados, and it is expected that British Honduras will reach the same stage in 1968. These developments have stemmed basically from changes in Britain's concepts of viability, following perhaps from a recognition that in a world of "super-powers" and international economic cooperation and aid, the traditional ideas of the independent nation-state have become outmoded.

At the opposite end of the scale, an equally clear-cut solution has been adopted by France, by integrating the Caribbean territories of Guadeloupe (which includes a number of smaller islands), Martinique, and French Guiana as departments of metropolitan France. Represented directly in the French legislature, these territories have the same voice in the affairs of France as have any other areas of comparable population, and their populace share the same basic obligations and benefits as other French citizens. This radical solution apparently derives from the French belief that the unifying force of French culture is stronger than the divisive forces of distance, climate, and race. Time may justify this faith. But at present it is difficult to resist the impression that the French islands have closer affinities with their Caribbean neighbors than with their European metropolis. It may be doubted whether the right to have a rather small say in French politics compensates for the inability to have much more than the same small say in the affairs of the French Caribbean. But opinion, both in France and in the French Caribbean, appears still to favor this solution, though it has many vocal critics.

In most of the remaining territories governmental responsibilities are shared between the unit and the metropolitan power in varying proportions. Broadly speaking, most internal matters are exclusive local responsibilities, and foreign affairs and defense are exclusive metropolitan responsibilities. In the British Caribbean, internal self-government, which in most British territories has become virtually complete, was seen as a relatively brief transitional stage on the way to independence. But in 1966 a new constitutional arrangement was made with Antigua, Dominica, Grenada, St. Kitts, St. Lucia, and St. Vincent, whereby Britain retained international responsibilities but provided for each of the island colonies to have full internal control, including constitutional amendment and the right to resolve unilaterally on complete independence. It seems possible that such a relationship might be indefinitely prolonged, and there are precedents for such an arrangement elsewhere in the Caribbean. The Netherlands Antilles and Surinam form two parts of the Tripartite Kingdom of the Netherlands. They have complete control over their internal affairs and a voice, along with the Netherlands metropolitan government, in the conduct of the foreign affairs and defense commitments of the Kingdom, each territory having a Minister-Plenipotentiary at the Hague, entitled to participate in meetings at the Dutch Cabinet when Kingdom affairs are being discussed. The arrangement appears to suit all parties, and may persist for some time, though the achievement of complete independence by Guyana has shown signs of stimulating neighboring Surinam to move in the same direction.

Perhaps less stable is the rather similar position of Puerto Rico, which controls its own internal affairs, has considerable benefits from association with the United States, but has virtually no control over defense or foreign policy, with only a Resident Commissioner in Washington, entitled to attend Congressional sessions as an observer. Both independence and assimilation, in the form of entering the American union as an additional state in the federation, have their strong advocates, but for the present the great majority of Puerto Ricans seem to prefer the existing relationship.

It is probable that, in most of these cases, such a relationship suits the Caribbean territory better than would complete independence, and it is possible that agitation for change may eventually come rather from the metropolitan countries than from the West Indies. Even if full internal self-government can be regarded as a possible permanent status, there remain some small and isolated problem territories. While the American Virgin Islands may conceivably aspire to a status similar to that of Puerto Rico, it may be wondered whether this could be practicable for the tiny British Virgin Islands, which are more closely connected with their American neighbors than with any British territory, or for the isolated Cayman Islands and the Turks and Caicos Islands, up to 1962 dependencies of Jamaica, but now on their own. Such unsolved constitutional problems are perhaps no more perplexing than some that have been "solved," such as the tiny island of St. Martin, its northern half being part of metropolitan France, with its departmental capital in Guadeloupe, and its southern half being part of the Netherlands Antilles, with its center in Curaçao, and a constituent of the Tripartite Kingdom of the Netherlands.

GOVERNMENT AND POLITICAL LIFE

Local constitutions tend to follow the respective metropolitan frameworks of government, without necessarily producing the same forms. In the independent British territories the basis is, as in Britain, a cabinet system with an elective lower house, from which ministers are drawn and to which they are responsible, with a Prime Minister as head of government and a Governor-General as titular head of state. The upper house is normally nominated, part by the Prime Minister and part by the Leader of the Opposition. While such a body cannot aspire to be much of an independent force in the legislature, it not only gives an opportunity to some people unable or unwilling to obtain election to be brought into political life, but also provides a safeguard for the various civil rights entrenched in the constitution, which cannot be altered by the government without the support of at least some of the opposition members. The Dutch territories also have cabinet systems, but their legislatures are unicameral, and constitutional safeguards are preserved by Kingdom control over major amendments. The situation in most British internally self-governing territories is broadly similar, though their powers of constitutional amendment are somewhat wider.

The constitution of Puerto Rico, on the other hand, is modeled on that of the United States. The Governor, popularly elected, is both head of state and head of the executive, and neither he nor his ministerial appointees may sit in the elected houses of the legislature. Both Senate and House of Representatives are directly elected; their functions are not very clearly distinguished, and the bifurcation of the legislature appears to serve little useful purpose. Many of the functions, such as the preparation of the budget, jealously guarded by the United States Congress, are, in Puerto Rico, performed by executive agencies, and the status of the legislature has been further decreased by the dominating position of the government party. In the French territories the government organs are those characteristic of a local rather than a national government.

In most territories all adults have the vote, and free elections are held regularly in accordance with the constitution in force. Political interest and participation are generally widespread, and polls are usually high. This has been largely due to the development of mass parties, often associated with labor unions, in the course of the agitation against metropolitan authorities for political advance. Parties have generally been organized to provide mass voting support for particular leaders, either of organized labor or of middle-class nationalist groups. Despite often elaborate constitutional organizations, many parties tend to be authoritarian in practice, and dependent for their success on charismatic leadership, which has often been reinforced by success in the anticolonial struggle.

In no major territory has any single party succeeded in emerging totally unchallenged, nor has the ideal of the one-party state been adopted, as it has in some parts of Africa. In the British territories personal rivalries among leaders and the traditional British concern for colonial minorities have ensured multiparty representation at constitutional conferences, and formal recognition has been given to a system of two or more parties—for example, by providing for opposition representation in upper houses. In the Dutch territories the adoption of the metropolitan form of proportional representation appears to have ensured the proliferation of parties. Of the major territories, Puerto Rico has perhaps come nearest to one-party dominance, but there the monolithic control of the ruling party has been somewhat offset by the special provision that, where minority parties fail to elect a third of the membership of either house, a number of additional seats are made available to them. While the promotion of this arrangement by the ruling party must be regarded as an act of remarkable political magnanimity, at the same time the weakness of the legislature in the Puerto Rican machinery of government makes this a relatively harmless and doubtless convenient gesture of conformity to the presumed two-party predilections of the American Congress.

West Indian political opinion has tended to be fairly consistent on questions of political advance, economic development, and increased social welfare, and party divisions have usually been based less on general principles of policy than on questions of personality. In Puerto Rico, however, the problem of the future relationship of the island with the United States has been the dominant distinguishing factor between parties, as were attitudes to the West Indian federation for a time in Jamaica, and possible future affiliations in British Honduras and other British territories. In Trinidad, Guyana, and Surinam, parties have tended to follow race lines and to represent predominantly persons either of African or of Asian origin. A two-party system on the British or American pattern can scarcely be said to be well established anywhere in the West Indies, although there are indications that Jamaica and some other territories are moving in that direction.

Political policy-making has been pragmatic rather than ideological, and conservative rather than radical. Responsible politicians have on the whole been rather reluctant to "rock the boat," and relatively little fundamental change has been attempted in existing economic or social structures. In part this has been attributable to behind-the-scenes cooperation between labor leadership and big business against more radical socializing policies, and in part because great reliance for further development has been placed on foreign investment, and it has thus been felt necessary to preserve a stable political and economic climate conducive to foreign confidence. Left-wing groups within certain parties have opposed such restraints on necessary reforms, but hitherto have been unable to produce a general conviction that such measures as nationalization of foreign assets, redistribution of internal wealth, and large-scale government enterprise offer more promising prospects than continued dependence on foreign trade, and a dominating, largely foreign-owned, private sector. Only in Guyana, where Marxist leadership coincided with the overwhelming dominance of a single foreign-owned private concern, have there been signs of the extreme type of colonial economic nationalism seen in other parts of the world, but even in that case public reaction to an austerity budget forced the government to back down.

Nationalism in general has taken harmless symbolic forms rather than brought about the radical reorientation many intellectuals feel essential for proper autonomous development. Politics remain circumscribed by local apprehensions about external realities to such an extent that many feel that self-government or independence has come in name only.

REGIONAL AND EXTERNAL RELATIONS

Rivalry rather than cooperation characterized the relations between the various parts of the Caribbean region until the formation, under the stress of war, of the Anglo-American Caribbean Commission in 1942, which concerned itself both with short-term emergency requirements of supply and communications, and with longer term research and development planning. In 1946 the other metropolitan powers, France and the Netherlands, joined in the organization, which, renamed the Caribbean Commission, functioned as an advisory and research body on a wide range of economic, social, and cultural matters. In 1959 the decision to transfer responsibility for such coordinating activities from the metropolitan to the local Caribbean governments met one of the main criticisms that had been leveled at the Commission, but did nothing about the other, the non-participation of the neighboring Latin American republics. The Caribbean Organization, which succeeded the Commission in 1961, was even further hampered by the non-participation of Jamaica and Trinidad, and lasted only until 1965, when it was apparently decided that an amalgam of departments of metropolitan France and territories with varying degrees of internal self-government was unworkable. Although a number of specialized regional bodies continues to exist, it seems unlikely that a more generalized organization can be formed without a closer approach to constitutional parity among its members. Even between the territories of individual metropolitan countries there are no formal political links. The French departments, the Netherlands Antilles and Surinam, Puerto Rico and the American Virgin Islands are administratively bound by quite separate links to the metropolitan center, as are the different British territories, though, of course, some groups of islands (e.g., St. Kitts-Nevis-Anguilla; Trinidad and Tobago; Guadeloupe and its dependencies, Marie-Galante, Désirade, Les Saintes, St. Bartélemy, and part of St. Martin; the Netherlands Antilles, consisting of Curaçao, Aruba, Bonaire, St. Eustatius, Saba, and the rest of St. Martin) fall into single administrative units. Even the short-lived federation of the West Indies did not include all the British territories in the area. This federation was preceded by a number of regional British enterprises, some of which—such as the University of the West Indies and an interisland shipping service—have survived its break-up. The region has also seen a number of bilateral and multilateral trading agreements, few of which have transcended old imperial boundaries, though since its independence Trinidad has held economic discussions with the Netherlands Antilles and Puerto Rico, as well as with Venezuela. However, the possibilities of regional economic cooperation between economies that are basically competing rather than complementary appear limited; only those territories which are completely independent have even legal freedom of action; and the history of the British federation seems to show that most territories felt that their prospects were better on their own than in combination with others.

None of the Caribbean territories has had full control of its external relations long enough to develop much of a foreign policy. Both Jamaica and Trinidad were admitted to the United Nations Organization immediately on attaining independence, and both countries have chosen to remain in the Commonwealth and have accepted various forms of aid from the United Kingdom, though some have felt this to be uncomfortably like a continuance of colonialism. Commonwealth links have also been fostered with Canada, as a more acceptable trading partner and source of aid than either the mother country or the United States, which is suspected of both racism and neo-imperialism. Anti-Americanism has been more marked in Trinidad, where it is exacerbated by the continued presence of a United States naval base, but even there it does not reach the rabid heights it does in many other parts of the world. Probably Trinidad's most important diplomatic activities have been lengthy and ultimately successful negotiations with her nearest neighbor, Venezuela, for the removal of a discriminatory trading duty levied from the 1880s, and Jamaica has shown diplomatic concern for the position of her citizens resident in the United Kingdom.

More vexatious have been the problems of the two British mainland territories, British Honduras, the subject of an irredentist claim from Guatemala, and Guyana, part of whose territory is claimed by Venezuela. Basically these claims, which are, as a matter of historical and legal fact, extremely weak, are against Britain rather than against the local governments (which have been associated with Britain in recent negotiations), and they are at variance with the expressed will of the populations of the territories concerned. It is unfortunate that these countries should have to face independence with such problems hanging over their heads.

For the region as a whole, external relations are a matter of attitudes rather than of diplomacy, and these have changed remarkably little with political advance. In general world affairs, the area still tends to look, through its metropolitan connections, to Europe or North America for a lead, making an occasional independent approving gesture toward African nationalism. There has been little or no connection with the Eastern power bloc, and, although neutralism has many sympathizers, much of the area appears firmly committed to the Western Alliance. Within the Western world, the area looks north rather than south, and despite the proximity of the South American continent, its attitudes to Latin America are largely those of Europe and North America. Little assessment has been made of the possibility of developing links with Latin America, although there are many pockets of West Indian migrants on the Caribbean littoral of South and Central America. Nor, except for territorial claims and ritual anticolonial utterances, have the West Indies impinged much on Latin American consciousness. The potential of the West Indies as a bridge between the North and South American continents has yet to be exploited.

It is evident from what has been said in this chapter that the West Indies show considerable social, economic, and political diversity, and that the whole area discussed, and even some of its individual territories, cannot be regarded as integrated. Yet it is equally evident that many similarities in social, economic, and political patterns and problems are to be found in the different parts of the region. It may be said that the various territories, diverse as they are, resemble each other more closely than any of them resemble any other places in the world, and it is possible that, if and when they succeed in emancipating themselves from social, cultural, economic, and political dependence on metropolitan countries, these resemblances in most essential points may become very close. In this sense one may perhaps talk coherently about the West Indies in general.

What is there that is distinctive and possibly significant about West Indian civilization? Most noteworthy perhaps in the world of today are the racial lessons to be learned from the West Indies. While it would be a gross exaggeration to suggest that the West Indies have solved racial problems, or that color counts for nothing in West Indian society, it is perhaps West Indians preeminently who have given the lie to Anglo-Saxon stereotypes about Negro inferiority and the perils of miscegenation, for they have enjoyed long contact with Western civilization, and, in recent years, relatively open opportunities irrespective of race. Jamaica, in particular, may be said to demonstrate that persons of African or Afro-European origin are capable of playing all the roles required for the working of an Anglo-Saxon type of civilization, without necessarily choosing to conform to all of its norms.

Another characteristic West Indian feature is smallness. There is in West Indian societies at least a potential for the evolution of close-knit, rather particularistic communities which may succeed in avoiding some of the rootlessness and anonymity which are causing so much concern to large advanced societies. A natural concomitant of smallness is lack of self-sufficiency and consequent international interdependence. Isolationism and inward-looking nationalism did not solve the problems of the first half of the twentieth century, and will not solve those of its second half. By establishing new criteria for independence, the West Indies may bring nearer a more realistic concept of the necessity for international interdependence between independent nations.

The hope of the West Indies that the world may change its ideas to suit them may seem impossibly optimistic, but irrational optimism is almost a precondition of West Indian existence. West Indians are inured to disaster and have learned to survive it. They are suspicious of the best laid schemes of men. When rational calculation suggests that economic development cannot hope to meet their rising expectations in the foreseeable future, their reaction is not to break themselves in attempting the impossible, but rather to hope for something to turn up. And something may. The British West Indies did not meet the old criteria for independence, but independence came. Perhaps the world may yet come to the view that it owes its people a living. Meanwhile obsession with the material side of life must not be allowed to make life not worth living. While most West Indians probably share the material desires of European and North American peoples, many of them are not thoroughly prepared to accept the materialist spirit which might make their satisfaction more possible. In the West Indies the business of living is not taken too seriously. Perhaps this is another lesson for a grim-faced world.

TWO

European Settlement

To all intents and purposes, West Indian history starts with Christopher Columbus. The pre-Columbian Amerindian inhabitants of the Caribbean area, unlike those of other parts of the American continents, had reached only an extremely primitive level of culture and social organization, and their influence on the subsequent history of the region was very slight. This influence, however, proved not unimportant in a rather negative way, as the nature and distribution of Amerindians affected the timing of conquest and settlement. But this was very much a subordinate factor to the aims and objectives of the Spanish colonizers. Whatever these may have been originally, early in the sixteenth century two requirements quickly came to override all others—precious metals and large, settled, productive, native populations, whose labor the conquerors could exploit to their profit and ease, while incidentally contributing to a third motive—the winning of souls for the Christian Church.

Columbus himself discovered many of the West Indian islands—the Bahamas on his first voyage, the northern part of the Lesser Antillean chain, Puerto Rico, and Jamaica on his second, Trinidad on his third. But neither he nor his immediate successors gave these nearly so much attention as the two largest islands which had been discovered on the first voyage, Hispaniola, which became the first center of Spanish power, and Cuba, its first important offshoot. It is true that Jamaica, thinly peopled by the mild and pacific Arawaks, was easily and even more thinly settled by the Spaniards in 1509, and that Puerto Rico, partly occupied by the fiercer Caribs, was conquered with a good deal more difficulty in the years immediately following. But neither of these had attained much population or development before the far more attractive possibilities of the mainland became evident with the conquest of Mexico in 1520, and were reinforced by the subsequent conquest of Peru. These sensational new discoveries, with their enormous mineral and human resources, admirably fulfilled the desires of Spanish colonists, and effectually diverted attention from the West Indian islands. New colonists by-passed the islands, old colonists left, development virtually ceased, and the West Indies came to have significance in the Spanish Empire less as colonies for their own sake than as defensive strongholds and staging posts on the way to and from the really important parts of the empire—Mexico, the isthmus of Panama, across which all trade with Peru and colonies farther south traveled, and, to a lesser extent, the Spanish Main, the Caribbean coast of the present-day republics of Colombia and Venezuela. This shift of the center of gravity of the Spanish Empire was a decisive factor in the early history of the West Indies. With the exception of Trinidad, which lies within sight of the Venezuelan mainland, further penetration of the islands of the Lesser Antilles, where there was little evidence of precious metals, and plenty of evidence of warlike Caribs, ceased; Jamaica and Puerto Rico remained insignificant, their small populations concerned mainly in the raising of cattle, pigs, and other foodstuffs for the supply of passing ships. In Hispaniola and Cuba, however, the effects, though serious, were cushioned to some extent, in the one case by a continued administrative significance, and in the other by an increasing strategic importance which derived from its position guarding the Florida channel, the best outlet from the Caribbean to Europe, as the Gulf Stream current to some extent offset the adverse northeast wind.

Spanish Monopoly

The territories covered by this study may be regarded as those considered of little value and consequently neglected by the Spaniards on account of their comparative poverty in bullion and tractable manpower. The Spanish impact on the later history of these territories, with the exception of Puerto Rico, which Spain managed to retain until the end of the nineteenth century, and, to a much lesser extent, Trinidad, which Spain lost a century earlier, was thus very limited. Spain's presence in the area had, however, more vital and lasting indirect effects. The decisive factor in the sixteenth-century Caribbean was the Spanish monopoly. Territorially this was based on the famous Papal Donation of 1493 (modified by the Treaty of Tordesillas with Portugal a year later), allocating to the Spanish Crown all areas, land and sea, to the west of a boundary set in the mid-Atlantic. Spanish monopoly was extended from ownership to exploitation by a comprehensive series of laws and regulations, which set up rigid controls over administration and settlement in the Indies, as well as over trade and communications with them, virtually confining these to a single Spanish port.

Thus from the outset foreigners were legally excluded from the Caribbean. Although some important individual exceptions were made, such concessions never vitiated the fundamental concept of the Indies as the exclusive province of the Crown of Castile. With the discovery of the riches of Mexico and Peru, the Spanish monopoly became a matter of international concern. Spain's European rivals and enemies became both jealous and apprehensive of the consequences of her new-found wealth; traders of other nations became conscious of the opportunities of markets inadequately supplied by the rigid Spanish system; and piratical raiders became aware of the chances of plunder of the rich return cargoes. The French, the English, and, above all, the Dutch, animated by hostility to Spain and hope of gain, began to frequent the Caribbean in defiance of the Spanish monopoly. Failure to obtain permission to trade peacefully led to concentration on clandestine commerce, and ultimately to outright raiding. The Spaniards responded vigorously to these threats by tightening their control over local authorities, by organizing an elaborate system of convoys, and by fortifying defensive positions in the Caribbean, especially Havana in Cuba, Cartagena on the Spanish Main, and San Juan in Puerto Rico. The second half of the sixteenth century saw Spain fairly successful locally in defending the monopoly. Although clandestine trade was not totally suppressed, it was always dangerous to the participants; although ships were cut out of convoys and captured, the great bulk of the treasure fleets regularly got through safely to Spain; and although coastal towns, including Cartagena, Santo Domingo, and San Juan, were sacked or held to ransom, the attackers could not occupy them permanently, and the real sources of Spanish wealth far in the mountains of the hinterland remained inviolate.

Spain was, however, less successful in Europe. King Philip II was unable to suppress the revolt of his Dutch subjects, to defeat Elizabethan England, or to establish a clear supremacy over France. Already in the 1520s the King of France had disputed his country's exclusion from the New World, and later in the century Protestant England argued against the validity of the Papal Donation. In European treaties, which brought about a short-lived general peace between Spain and her enemies at the turn of the century, Spain was unable to obtain the acceptance by other powers of her monopolistic claims, and was having to face the argument that these could only be recognized when they had been backed up by effective occupation. The decline of Spain's power in Europe, which continued apace throughout the seventeenth century, had inevitable consequences in weakening her position in the Indies, and was the basic factor in the seventeenth-century transformation of the Caribbean area from a Spanish preserve to a zone of quadripartite European colonial rivalry.

Non-Hispanic Settlements

The location of non-Hispanic settlements in the West Indies is to be explained primarily by the pattern of earlier Spanish colonizing activities. The first efforts of the northern European nations were made in those areas where Spain not only had no effective possession, but also did not have strong claims—the mainland of North America was one such area, and another was Guiana, the debatable land of the "Wild Coast" between the mouths of the Orinoco, indisputably Spanish, and of the Amazon, decidedly in the Portuguese sphere of influence. The next move was to the Lesser Antilles, where Spanish claims were stronger but possession not established. A little later the British were able to move into the Belize area of the Bay of Honduras, an inhospitable and unexploited tract, distant from any seat of Spanish jurisdiction and not falling clearly under the responsibility of either Yucatan or Guatemala; and in the second half of the century it was possible for even occupied territory to be wrested from Spain—Jamaica by the British, and Saint-Domingue, the western part of the island of Hispaniola, by the French.

The nature of these non-Hispanic settlements, however, derived rather from varying metropolitan factors. The presence of the Dutch in the West Indies is partly to be explained by the carrying of the war for independence from Spain into the Caribbean. But economic factors were also of significance, for the union of Portugal and Spain in 1580 deprived the Dutch of the use of Portuguese sources of the salt vital for their fisheries, and an alternative source was found in the Araya saltpans of Venezuela, and later in Curaçao. By the early seventeenth century, with the remarkable upsurge of Dutch mercantile activities, new areas of expansion were being sought for the carrying trade, and new outposts for a trading empire. The Caribbean offered opportunities for clandestine trade with the Spanish colonies, and the establishment of Dutch or other non-Hispanic colonies could generate further trade. The Dutch West India Company, formed with strong government backing in 1621, ensured unity of purpose and coordination of effort. By the second quarter of the century Dutch shipping dominated the sea-lanes of the Caribbean, a process accelerated by the Dutch capture of the entire Spanish treasure fleet in 1628.

It was largely through the replacement of hostile Spanish by friendly Dutch control in the area that the English and French were able to set up their first Caribbean colonies, which in their early years were heavily dependent on Dutch shipping for supplying their necessities and taking their produce to European markets. Dutch supremacy in the Caribbean might have been more enduring had they directed more of their efforts there, and less to Brazil, part of which they had seized from the Spanish-dominated Portuguese in the 1620s, only to be ousted again in the 1650s. Although the Dutch established an enduring settlement in Guiana in 1616, their main interest was in trade rather than in colonization, and their other important acquisition, Curaçao, was taken from Spain, less for its productive possibilities, though its salt was of some importance. than for its admirable situation for commercial penetration of the Spanish Main.

English motives were similarly mixed. There was strong anti-Spanish sentiment evident, not only in the expeditions of Drake in the 1580s, but also in the activities of the Puritan promoters of the colony of Old Providence off the Nicaraguan coast, conveniently in the path of Spanish shipping homeward bound from Panama. This was a settlement in which cultivation was quickly abandoned in favor of illicit trade and plunder of Spanish vessels, until it was retaken by Spain in 1641. Oliver Cromwell's "Western Design," which resulted in the English conquest of Jamaica in 1655, was motivated by the same hostile feeling toward Spain, and, at least in its early years as a British colony, Jamaica was thought of primarily as a base for the development of trading links with Spanish America. But most early English enterprise, first in Guiana, and, as a by-product of activity there, in the Lesser Antilles, was concerned more with settlement. The promoters, who were commercial rather than governmental, were concerned with raising products for European markets and were able to take advantage of the great wave of English migration of the 1620s to the 1640s, deriving partly from economic and partly from religious conditions in England, and resulting in the peopling of colonies on the North American mainland as well as in the West Indies. The main attraction for the English emigrant was land, and thousands were prepared to pay for their passages by binding themselves to work in the colonies as indentured servants for a period of three to seven years, after which they became free to take up land of their own. In the early years the main crop in the British colonies was tobacco; the individual land holding was small and was worked by the owner with the aid of a handful of indentured servants for whose maintenance he was responsible. Metropolitan support came principally from the mercantile circles of London rather than from the government, but some form of royal grant or sanction, particularly in confirmation of land tenure arrangements, was also necessary if a colony was to be placed on a sound basis. This led to some confusion, as different groups obtained permission to colonize some of the same islands, and ultimately a struggle ensued between competing mercantile interests, operating behind competing court noblemen, for influence with the Crown and its advisers, and the resulting tangle of claims was not finally sorted out until the 1660s. Permanent British settlement in the West Indies, however, dates from the 1620s. Various earlier attempts made on the Guiana coast were short-lived, and the first successful settlement was made on St. Kitts, which in its early years was shared with a group of French settlers, who sensibly cooperated with the English against Carib threats. Barbados was discovered a year or two later and quickly became the most important colony, boasting some 30,000 inhabitants by 1640. Its rapid development was assisted by the total absence of Amerindians and its easy terrain, and some of the inevitable difficulties of the early years were lessened by the availability of dyewoods on the island, which could be immediately exploited to bring in a quick cash return. Although the Spaniards dispersed the St. Kitts colony in 1629, it was soon reoccupied, and British settlement had extended to Nevis, Antigua, and Montserrat by 1632.

French colonizing activity was determined rather more by political, and rather less by economic, motives. The French quest for trade was less urgent than that of the Dutch, and commercial capital was less readily available for colonial enterprises. The French thirst for land was less pressing than that of the English; labor was more difficult to come by, and more attractive terms had to be offered to the French *engagé* than to the English indentured servant. Nevertheless, there were enterprising individuals interested in colonization, and they were able to play on the anti-Spanish proclivities of the government of Cardinal Richelieu to obtain official support, and the capital that mercantile sources were slow to invest. After early and unsuccessful efforts in Guiana (although these eventually led to the settlement of Cayenne, it never developed into an important colony), the French established themselves in St. Kitts along with the English in the 1620s, and in the 1630s started the settlement of Guadeloupe and Martinique. Though delayed by the presence of a Carib population, developments on these French islands followed similar lines to those in the English colonies.

THE SUGAR REVOLUTION

The non-Hispanic colonies had scarcely been founded before their entire character began to undergo a rapid transformation. It soon proved that tobacco, which was their main crop, could compete neither in quality nor in quantity with that of Virginia, and the glut that presently occurred on the European market hit West Indian producers. But the Dutch, who were closely interested in the prosperity of the British and French West Indian islands, were ready with an alternative crop, sugar cane, which they had learned to cultivate and process during their occupation of Portuguese Brazil. Sugar was not entirely new to the West Indies, for it was cultivated from the early sixteenth century in Hispaniola, and introduced into Puerto Rico. But the industry failed to develop, partly owing to lack of capital and labor once new areas of the Spanish empire were opened up, and by the seventeenth century production had declined to a scarcely significant level. European demand, however, was rapidly increasing, largely due to the introduction of tea and coffee (thought to be undrinkable without sweetening), and could only be met from the tropics, as sugar cane could not be grown successfully in temperate climates and the potentialities of sugar beet were not then known in Europe. During the decade of the 1640s the profitability of sugar was found to be much greater than that of tobacco, or indeed any other crop, and it was widely adopted in the Lesser Antilles, with the Dutch supplying the plants, and, in some cases, the capital and the experienced personnel, and even, in Martinique, a large body of refugee settlers from Brazil.

The consequences of this change were so rapid and far-reaching as to justify the use of the term "the sugar revolution" for the process. The basic cause of change was the nature of the conditions required for sugar production. Sugar cane must be converted into sugar through a complicated process of milling, boiling, and crystallizing immediately after it has been cut. It cannot be transported or stored before processing. Thus sugar production is necessarily an industrial as well as an agricultural operation, demanding coordination of cutting and milling. The achievement of the necessary cooperation between field and factory is made more difficult by the markedly seasonal maturing of the cane crop and by the fact that the manufacture of sugar can only be carried out economically on a fairly large scale. From the outset the solution to this problem was to have relatively large production units with the raising of the cane and the manufacture of sugar under the same ownership and management, the typical early plantation consisting of between 200 and 300 acres of cane field feeding a single factory, and employing during the crop time a large, unskilled labor force in the heavy work of cane-cutting. These were very different requirements from those of tobacco growing, where small-scale units of under thirty acres were perfectly viable, and indeed desirable, as the individual plants (unlike sugar cane) needed careful attention. The introduction of sugar thus entailed a radical change in the distribution of land, from a large number of small holdings to a small number of large holdings. As land values rose with the greater profitability of sugar, the wealthier were able to buy out the poorer and consolidate their holdings into large estates. Because of the problem of transporting cane to the factory, the economic size of an individual estate was limited, but many planters came to own more than one estate. Soon all the best land was parceled out among large proprietors. The capital required for large-scale acquisition, and for the construction of sugar factories, meant that sugar was essentially a rich man's crop.

This raised difficulties of labor supply. Few of the dispossessed small-holders (who in Barbados numbered some 12,000 leaving the island divided among some seven or eight hundred great proprietors) stayed to work for wages on the sugar plantations. They drifted into urban occupations, emigrated to try their luck in other colonies in the West Indies or North America, or took to the sea as fishermen or buccaneers. The flow of indentured servants which had provided the small proprietors with a temporary labor force soon dried up. Not only was the regimented, unskilled work of a sugar plantation particularly uncongenial, but the only real incentive had been the possibility of setting up as proprietors on their own land after working out their indenture. In a sugar economy the scale of capital required to set up on one's own was quite beyond the means of such settlers, and in any case the available land was quickly engrossed by the large planters. The West Indies could no longer exercise the attractive power of a "frontier" society with open opportunities for economic advancement.

Voluntary indenture was for some years partly replaced by various forms of forced emigration from Europe. Transportation as a legal penalty produced some unwilling immigrants; in the ports of England and France it became not uncommon for people to be virtually seized off the streets and shipped out, and during the English Civil Wars prisoners on the losing side were often sent to people the West Indian colonies. But the political and social conditions in Europe were not such as to produce a large, steady supply of involuntary labor, and the numbers obtained in these ways could not meet the apparently insatiable demands of the planters. Again, however, the Dutch were ready with an alternative, the Negro slave. When the Dutch had conquered northern Brazil they had also taken over some of the Portuguese slave-trading stations in West Africa, and as they began to lose their grip on Brazil a fresh market for slaves became desirable. Indeed, it is probable that one of the reasons for their stimulation of sugar cultivation in the West Indies was the expectation that it would generate traffic for their ships, not only in sugar and general supplies, but also in slaves. Negro slaves had been introduced to the West Indies in the early years of Spanish colonization, particularly as a labor force for sugar production, but they accounted for only a small proportion of the population, even in the colonies where they were most numerous. The situation soon became very different in the Lesser Antilles, where the Negro slaves quickly began to outnumber the European colonists.

This shift from a European to an African labor force with the introduction of sugar is primarily to be explained in terms of availability, the political and social situation in West Africa favoring the export of enslaved labor. This greater availability was reflected in costs. It was often cheaper to buy the labor of an African for life than of a European for a comparatively few years. Other factors may have also played some part. Europeans were believed to be, and possibly were, more susceptible than Africans to tropical diseases, and worse equipped for arduous, disciplined field work in a hot climate. But it should be noted that the mortality among

Africans as well as Europeans in the West Indies was very high, and that the previous style of life of many slaves transported from Africa can have borne no closer relation than that of the Europeans to what faced them in the West Indies. It is possible also that planters felt that European convicts, many of whom were not transported for life, and whose labor was thus available only for the duration of their sentences, formed a less stable basis for a labor force than Africans, whose slave status was permanent, and whose children born in slavery would be available to follow after them. But it seems likely that mortality was regarded as a more important cause of labor force instability than status. The planters may further have thought that Europeans, once freed of their obligations, might be difficult to fit into a plantation society, and so create a social problem, although the difficulties thus created could hardly have been on the scale of the acute problem of social, and often physical, control posed by the alienation between the European owners and the permanently enslaved Africans. There may also have been among European owners less compunction about the holding in bondage of Africans than of people of their own race. But the treatment of white bondsmen rather suggests that any inhibitions were more likely to have been legal than moral, and, on the other hand, the concept of the African race as natural slaves appears to have been less a cause than a consequence of slavery. Whatever the preferences of planters may have been, they probably had relatively little effect. The West Indies needed labor and took what was offered. Very soon after the conversion to sugar production, what was offered was overwhelmingly Negro in race and slave in status. Thus it was that the coming of sugar transformed not only the economic basis of the non-Hispanic West Indian colonies, but their ethnic composition and their social system as well.

METROPOLITAN AND INTERNATIONAL RELATIONS

These consequences were far-reaching enough, but the sugar revolution also contributed less directly to other changes. In particular, it enhanced the value of West Indian colonies, and so increased the interest of the European metropolitan countries in their possessions in the area, an interest which ultimately resulted in the evolution of West Indian policies by England and France. The main tendency of these policies was to bring the colonies under the direct economic and political control of the mother country. Up to the 1650s the leading settlers in the English colonies and the appointed governors in the French colonies had been subject to very little effective control from the home governments in Europe, and, economically, the colonies were dependent much more on the Dutch than on their own nationals.

In 1651 the Commonwealth government in England, hostile to the Dutch for a variety of reasons, passed the famous Navigation Act, restricting most trade with English colonies to English shipping. Though aimed primarily at the Dutch carrying trade, the implications of this policy (which was subsequently developed in a number of other measures, such as those which stipulated that most trade with the colonies must pass through the mother country, irrespective of the ultimate origin or destination of the goods) were to create an exclusive, self-sufficient imperial system, designed to be conducive both to the security of the mother country, by stimulating its maritime power, and to its prosperity, by expanding its trade. A series of Anglo-Dutch wars in the third quarter of the seventeenth century failed to move the English from their commitment to this policy, which became more practicable as English shipping expanded.

Defiance of the Navigation Act by Barbados, which remained Royalist in sympathy after the Parliamentary triumph in the English Civil Wars of the 1640s, and continued trading with the Dutch, brought about direct political intervention by the Commonwealth government, which sent out a fleet in 1652 to bring the West Indian colonies under its authority. Nor was this all. The development of an anti-Dutch policy had not mitigated traditional anti-Spanish sentiments, at least on the part of Lord Protector Cromwell, who sent out under direct government auspices an expedition specifically aimed at capturing West Indian territory from Spain. Failing miserably at its original objective, Santo Domingo, the expedition went on to capture Jamaica in 1655, though sporadic Spanish resistance was not finally subdued until 1660. By that time monarchical government had been restored in England, giving an opportunity for a reconsideration of the status of colonial possessions. There was little difficulty over Jamaica, which had fallen to an expedition of regular national forces and was thus deemed to be at the absolute disposal of the government. The other colonies, however, had been settled by promoters operating under various royal charters. It was decided to extinguish the rights of these grantees, and bring these colonies too under the direct authority of the Crown. The local Assemblies, represesentative of the settlers and with the power to vote local taxes, which had developed in the early years, were, however, confirmed, and one was set up in Jamaica, where it was hoped to attract settlers, who, it was feared, might not come to the new colony if there was not provision for such an institution to protect their rights and liberties.

Developments in the French islands, though somewhat later, were very similar in effect. During the ministry of Colbert in the 1660s and 1670s, a series of regulations provided for the monopolization by France of the trade and shipping of the French West Indian colonies—measures which the Dutch were forced to acquiesce in after the Franco-Dutch wars. At this time too, the administration of the French islands came directly under the Crown, which appointed governors, primarily responsible for military affairs, and *intendants,* who controlled civil administration. While the settlers had some influence over the local conduct of government, they had no representative institutions with taxing and lawmaking powers, such as existed in the English colonies.

The principal effect of these moves was to squeeze the Dutch out of the dominating position they had held in the trade of the non-Hispanic Caribbean. While the British and French exclusive systems were never completely effective in their operation, and clandestine trade with the Dutch continued, the effect on the Dutch position in the West Indies was marked. The formidable Dutch West India Company collapsed in bankruptcy in 1674, and although Dutch possessions in Guiana were extended by the acquisition of Surinam, which had been settled by the English in the 1650s and was ceded to the Dutch in 1667, the Netherlands government's interest remained more in trade than in colonization, and was directed less and less toward the Caribbean, as opportunities there diminished with the growing ability of the French and English to handle the trade of their own possessions.

The problem of Dutch economic preponderance was not the only one facing England and France in the middle of the century. Although their colonies had been established and developed, they had not been recognized by Spain, which still claimed exclusive rights to the whole area, with the exception of the Netherlands Antilles. (Spain had had to concede Dutch ownership of these islands, along with Dutch independence from Spain, in 1648.) The decline of Dutch naval power in the Caribbean, which English and French policy was bringing about, left these nations to face the Spaniards themselves. Neither England nor France had in the seventeenth century a strong enough navy to match Spain in the West Indies, and both resorted to the use of irregular forces for this purpose. The unsettled conditions of the early seventeenth century and the opportunities of plunder in the area had given rise to groups of piratical adventurers, known as buccaneers, whose numbers were augmented by the dispossession of small settlers after the sugar revolution. From their main base in the small island of Tortuga, off the northwest coast of Hispaniola, they attacked Spanish shipping and raided coastal settlements. Tortuga was brought under French control in the 1650s, and the buccaneers were given official sanction to operate as privateers against the Spaniards in the service of the French Crown. After the capture of Jamaica by the English, buccaneers were also welcomed there on the same basis, and under the leadership of Sir Henry Morgan numerous damaging raids were carried out on the Spanish mainland. Buccaneering activity not only coerced Spain but also resulted in further non-Hispanic colonization. From their vantage point in Tortuga, the French were able to penetrate the western part of Hispaniola and establish their colony of Saint-Domingue, which Spain was slow to recognize but unable to reconquer. In Central America other haunts of the buccaneers in the Bay of Honduras and the Bay of Campeche developed into logwood-cutting establishments, as the buccaneers found it more profitable to go ashore and cut the valuable dye-wood themselves than to plunder Spanish ships carrying it. Although the Spaniards drove the logwood-cutters from Campeche in the early eighteenth century, the British establishments in the Bay of Honduras were more or less permanently occupied from the 1660s, to develop ultimately into the colony of British Honduras.

Official support for privateering had paid off for the British by 1670, when the Spaniards agreed to recognize the English settlements in the West Indies in return for British agreement to suppress the buccaneers. This was far from being an unacceptable *quid pro quo*, as the buccaneers had proved a very mixed blessing. In the Second Dutch War of 1665-67 they had been reluctant and ineffective in moving against Britain's enemies, the French and the Dutch, preferring to attack the Spaniards, with whom the English were then at peace. Moreover, the British were now becoming anxious to establish better relations with Spain, and more peaceful conditions in the Caribbean generally, in the hope of being able to obtain Spanish agreement, or at least connivance, to trade between Jamaica and the Spanish colonies. Toward the end of the century such trade, probably more clandestine than authorized, did develop, and its expansion remained an important object of British West Indian policy.

France, denied recognition of her possession of Saint-Domingue (which was not fully accepted by Spain until 1697), continued using the buccaneers for some time longer. But in 1684, partly under pressure from the Dutch and the English, and partly in the hope of improving relations with Spain in view of the looming question of the succession to the Spanish monarchy, France also agreed to suppress buccaneering. Privateering activity now became confined to times of formal war between the European powers, and the buccaneers, denied official warrant for their activities, became, if they persisted in them, simply pirates, outlawed by all nations including their own. The putting down of piracy in the West Indies was a slow process, but by the end of the seventeenth century the situation in the Caribbean was much more stable.

Spain had reluctantly agreed to accept a partition of the area among various European powers, and to abandon her exclusive claims. Dutch power in the Caribbean had waxed and waned. The English and French, having been able to establish themselves in the West Indies through the anti-Spanish activities and the direct aid of the Dutch, had turned on their benefactors and excluded them from much of the area. The two emergent powers, cooperative in their early weakness over, for example, the sharing of St. Kitts, had already come to blows in the war of 1665-67, when the French had conquered and devastated the British Leeward Islands; and Anglo-French rivalry, which was to be such a dominant factor in the history of many parts of the world in the eighteenth century, had already become apparent in the Caribbean.

THREE

Sugar and Slavery

In the late seventeenth century there developed in the West Indian islands an economy based on sugar production and a society based on slavery, which lasted until well into the nineteenth century. In most of the territories covered by this study sugar had, by the end of the eighteenth century, become much the most important product, and Negro slaves much the most important element in the population.

The Sugar Economy

The requirements of sugar cane cultivation set the pattern of the economy. The first of these was fertile land, which was far from abundant. The total land area of the West Indian islands is not great, and much of it is mountainous or otherwise unsuitable for estate cultivation. Moreover, in the long run, constant sugar cropping diminishes the fertility of the land, and this, under eighteenth-century conditions, led to reduced yields and increased costs of production, through, for example, having to plant out canes afresh, instead of leaving the old roots to ratoon. The steadily increasing European demand in this period called for a great expansion of sugar production which was achieved primarily by the extension of cultivation to new lands, and these, being often virgin soils, tended to have cost advantages over the older colonies. The expansion, however, did not develop quite into a moving "frontier" of sugar cultivation, largely owing to the political fragmentation of the area into exclusive imperial spheres of trade and settlement.

The land problem was most acute in the British possessions. By the early eighteenth century the very small islands of Barbados, Antigua, St. Kitts, and Nevis had more or less reached the limit of economic exploitation, and were beginning to incur higher production

49

costs. At this time British demand for a product that was still something of a luxury could be satisfied from British colonial production, with a surplus for re-export to other European countries. But, as demand increased, it had to be met out of sugar expansion in the later developed, but very much larger, island of Jamaica. By the latter part of the century Jamaica, too, was beginning to experience diminishing returns, and the West Indies were failing to satisfy the higher level of British domestic demand, and failing even more to provide a surplus for re-export. The British might have tried to acquire further sugar lands through successful warfare against the possessions of other European powers, but this was never an important object of the numerous British campaigns of the eighteenth-century wars, largely due to the fact that the vested interests in the existing British islands feared competition from lower-cost producing areas. Their influence probably contributed to the abandonment of projects for the annexation of the undeveloped Spanish island of Puerto Rico, and to the return of the developed French sugar islands of Guadeloupe and Martinique after their capture in the Seven Years War. The territories which were acquired and retained at that time—Tobago, Grenada, St. Vincent, and Dominica—posed much less of a threat to existing interests. They were virtually undeveloped (indeed, the two last named had until then been largely left in Carib hands by both British and French) and their mountainous terrain offered little likelihood of speedy low-cost exploitation. Although they soon did begin to contribute a little to British West Indian sugar output, Tobago went back to the French after the next war, and in general these territories could not be expected to remedy the British problem of underproduction. Not until the nineteenth century did the restrictionist attitude of the British sugar interests cease to prevail over demands for cheaper and more abundant sugar.

Although the French islands developed more slowly than the British, their potential was much greater. Guadeloupe and Martinique, the largest of the Lesser Antilles, were much bigger than the British islands in that area, and by the middle of the century were providing larger crops probably at lower cost than their British neighbors. In 1760 the admission to the British sugar market of the crop of captured Guadeloupe brought about a drastic fall in prices. But much more important to the French was Saint-Domingue (two-and-a-half times the size of the largest British island, Jamaica) which rapidly developed in the second half of the century to become the world's largest producer, with an output almost as large as that of all the British West Indian territories combined.

Of the remaining territories covered by this study, only the Dutch mainland colonies in Guiana, where exploitation of the coastal area was made possible by the application of the metropolitan technique of empoldering tidal land, became at all significant in sugar production in the eighteenth century. Conditions of soil or climate were for the most part unsuitable in the Dutch Antilles, the Bahamas, and a number of the smaller islands of the Lesser Antilles. In the British wood-cutting settlements in the Bay of Honduras insecurity from Spanish attack made plantation agriculture impracticable, and it was later prohibited in treaties which regularized the settlers' position. The Spanish islands of Puerto Rico and Trinidad were the major territories whose sugar potential was neglected in the eighteenth century. This is principally to be attributed to the inability of Spain to supply the initiative, the capital, or the market required for a flourishing sugar industry, and to Spanish adherence to the exclusive imperial system. Not until these policies began to be modified at the end of the century, by the admission of French settlers to Trinidad and the opening of Puerto Rico to the trade of other nations, was there much possibility of fuller exploitation, and not until the nineteenth century did these become sugar islands.

As we have already seen, the "sugar revolution" made it virtually impossible for the West Indies to attract a free European labor force, and this led to the substitution of African slave labor. The exploitation of sugar land was thus dependent upon the availability of Negro slaves. Slaves were at first supplied by the Dutch, but the adoption of exclusive imperial trade policies by the English and French implied their entry into the African slave trade themselves, in order to preserve this important branch of the trade of their West Indian colonies for their own nationals. By the end of the seventeenth century both the British and the French empires were virtually self-sufficient in slaves. Ships were sailing from Bristol, Nantes, and other ports for the African coast, where they bartered manufactures, firearms, and liquor for slaves, whom they then transported to the West Indian colonies for sale to the planters, often in exchange for sugar, which they could then carry back to Europe. Although the potential profits were very high if a good bargain

could be made on each of the three legs of the triangular traffic, the
risks were also considerable. Political and economic conditions in
West Africa were not stable, and gluts of European goods could
quickly arise, or heavy bribes become necessary to carry on trade.
The "middle passage" from Africa to the West Indies was always
hazardous. Losses of part of the slave cargo from disease were
frequent, and if some particularly virulent outbreak occurred, or if
the voyage was prolonged by bad weather and drinking water ran
short, the losses might be almost total. In the West Indies there
might be no cargoes for Europe to be had. As the planters never
seemed to have any ready money, the slaves would have to be disposed of on credit, and plantation debts often turned out to be
bad ones. Difficulties such as these reduced the Royal African Company, which was set up with a monopoly of the English slave trade
in 1672, to desperate straits within fifteen years. Yet the trade always continued to attract plenty of investors until its suppression in
the nineteenth century, largely because, among the many uncertainties, one thing always seemed sure—there would be a demand for slaves from the West Indian planters at all times. This
constant demand was a significant feature of the slave trade, which
was not confined to areas where cultivation was expanding. It was
not the case that once an adequate labor force was established in
the West Indies the trade could fall off. Even established plantations in established colonies required constant replenishments of
their labor force in the form of new slaves from Africa, for the
slaves did not succeed in maintaining their numbers in the West
Indies by natural increase.

This was due at least in part to conditions inherent in slavery.
The death rate among slaves was probably higher than among other
immigrant groups in the West Indies. One contributing factor was
malnutrition, which could result from short-sighted economy or
simple meanness on the part of the owner, on whom, of course,
fell the expense of feeding his slaves. Another contributory factor
was overwork. Especially in crop-time, slaves would often be driven
beyond reasonable limits. Physical resistance to the diseases always prevalent in the eighteenth-century Caribbean might be further lowered by exposure to damp, through inadequate housing or
having to work ill-clothed in the rain; and psychological resistance
could be undermined by despair at slave conditions generally, which
in numerous cases led even healthy slaves to suicide. In any case,
death rates would still have been high in this period without these

additional factors. But it seems likely that the other restriction on natural increase, low birth rates, must be explained primarily by slave conditions. In the earlier years particularly, the planters' demand was for men rather than women, and two or three times as many males as females were transported. This in itself made for a low birth rate. But even when, in the later years of slavery, the sex ratio became more even, birth rates remained low. Malnutrition and overwork among slave women, no doubt, was part of the cause. But the slaves also seem to have shown some aversion to breeding in captivity, and the planters too gave little encouragement to slave-breeding at least until late in the eighteenth century. It was reckoned to be more economic to employ female slaves in field labor than in raising a new generation of slaves, and cheaper to purchase adult slaves from Africa, even though nearly half of those might be expected to die within a year or two in spite of careful "seasoning" to their new environment, than to raise to maturity on the plantations slave children, less than half of whom could be expected to live to the age of five. It was thus essential for the planters to have regular recourse to the slave market to maintain the strength of their labor forces.

Within the plantation economy, the slaves are perhaps more properly regarded as a form of capital equipment than as a substitute for wage labor. The biggest problem of a slave force as a capital asset was its often rapid depreciation through mortality, and the constant need for renewal. If a plantation was unable, because of hard times or simply bad management, to make good its losses for a few years, the slave force could become so run down that the plantation could not be operated efficiently, and very heavy capital outlays on new slaves would be needed to restock it with an adequate supply of workers. Another problem was that the slave force had to be large enough to meet the peak demands for labor during crop-time, but during the rest of the year, when much less labor was needed, the full slave strength still had to be housed, fed, and clothed at the plantation's expense. Moreover, under such a highly paternalistic system individual productivity tended to be low, as there was little incentive to work more than the minimum necessary to escape punishment. All estates, too, generally had to carry a relatively unproductive element consisting of the aged, the infirm, and the young. On the other hand, such a form of capital investment was not without advantages. Slaves could be employed on a wide variety of different tasks as plantation needs arose, and could be trained for a number of highly skilled forms of work on the estate, as blacksmiths, coopers, carpenters, sugar-boilers, and the like. The existence of such a hierarchy of jobs, more responsible and less uncongenial than field labor, also provided some rudimentary incentive to industry and good behavior. Moreover, unlike land or factory equipment, slaves were a relatively liquid form of capital which could be moved from one place to another with their owner, or readily realized by sale. Indeed, the slave force often came to be the most valuable capital item of a sugar estate, so much so that estates were sometimes purchased entire, simply with a view to obtaining the slaves, whom the purchaser could then move onto his understocked plantation. Toward the end of the eighteenth century when, in some places, estates often found themselves without enough slaves, enterprising individuals who did not own plantations built up gangs of slaves, which they hired out to estates for task work; but in general ownership of approximately one slave per acre of cane field was regarded as essential to the smooth-working prosperity of a sugar plantation.

Apart from the initial outlay involved in the establishment of the West Indian colonies, which was furnished from European mercantile sources, most of the capital subsequently required for the expansion or rehabilitation of the sugar industry appears to have come, through one channel or another, from the profits of sugar itself. Much of the opening up of new areas or islands was accomplished by settlers from the older sugar colonies which did not offer so good a field for further investment. Credit was also available from sugar merchants, but it is probable that their loanable funds were derived from previous profitable operations in sugar. Credit was needed for the purchase of slaves as well as for expansion, for few planters in fact seem to have managed to make good their losses regularly out of annual profits, but rather to have bought relatively large numbers of slaves at infrequent intervals, generally requiring loans to make such purchases. In the British islands these loans normally came from the sugar factors in England, to whom the planters consigned their crops for marketing, and through whom they normally obtained such European goods as they required to have shipped out. The factor would recoup himself for advances, with commission and interest, out of proceeds of the sale of the planter's sugar. As high rates of interest were charged on loans to the West Indies, the loans tended to accumulate unless they were immediately paid off, and, especially in the later years of the eighteenth century, much of the profit from sugar cultivation was finding its way into the pocket of the factor rather than of the planter. In the French islands it was more normal for sugar to be sold locally to resident merchants in the West Indies than for planters to consign it for sale on commission in France, and supplies from Europe were also obtained through these local merchants rather than directly. It was thus the local rather than the metropolitan merchant who became the main source of planters' credit.

It is difficult to generalize about the profitability of sugar planting. Much depended on European price levels which fluctuated considerably, especially in time of war, but without sharing the general upward tendency of costs, which rose due to soil exhaustion, increases in the price of slaves, and the growing burdens of debt. Thus profit margins probably declined in the course of the eighteenth century. Yet it is likely that plantations continued to be capable of showing satisfactory profits, provided they were properly managed. Often, however, they were not. Many planters were absentee owners who not only demanded returns from their estates to maintain their establishments in Europe, when these should have been ploughed back into the estate, but whose very absence often meant slacker management, or at least less attention to the owner's best interests. Even a capable resident planter would soon be in difficulties if he did not succeed in steering clear of debt. The diminishing attractiveness of sugar growing, especially in the British islands, is seen in the increasing difficulty experienced at the end of the eighteenth century in finding purchasers for sugar estates. Long before the end of slavery the industry was ceasing to provide many of the planters with the level of profit which they considered they should be able to expect.

The mobilizing of land, labor, and capital, and the deploying of these factors for the profitable production of sugar, were not the only economic problems the planters had to face. In order to produce sugar at all it was necessary to keep the labor force alive by feeding it. This common problem was approached in a number of ways on different islands at various times. Most planters were naturally reluctant to use any potential sugar land for the growing of food crops, preferring to obtain food supplies for their slaves from outside their estates, either locally or by importation. In the earlier years local purchases of grain or vegetable crops could be made in some territories from small farmers, but these tended to decline in numbers. In any case this source could seldom fill all needs. In particular, meat, fish, and wheat flour had to be imported from outside the Caribbean. Importation of food had the disadvantage that supplies from Europe were expensive, not always regular, and liable to be completely disrupted in war time.

The British islands, however, soon found a more convenient source in the North American mainland colonies, which, by the end of the seventeenth century, were producing food surpluses and were well placed to exploit the Newfoundland Banks for the most significant imported food item, salt fish. In addition, North America could supply another perennial need, lumber, required for building and containers for shipping sugar. A great intercolonial trade soon sprang up, financed and organized by the New England merchants and shipowners, and became vital to the West Indian islands. In general the planters paid for these American imports with the by-products of sugar production, rum and molasses. Nor was this trade confined to the British West Indies; for, although it was illegal, the French were usually only too glad to obtain American supplies in exchange for otherwise unsaleable molasses, which they were not allowed to distill into rum as that might compete with the mother country's brandy. As the British planters normally found it more profitable to make rum than to sell raw molasses, the Americans, who had distilleries in New England to serve the frontier and the Indian trade, often preferred to trade with the French than the British. The Molasses Act, which passed the British Parliament in 1733, largely at the behest of the British West Indian interests, was designed to put a stop to this extra-imperial trade, and to protect the supplies to the British islands, but it was never very effective. After the American Revolution, despite pleas from the West Indians, the shipping of the new United States was virtually excluded from the British West Indies. American supplies could be imported only in British ships, and this raised prices, as did the use of alternative sources within the British Empire, such as Ireland and the remaining British colonies in North America. As imported supplies thus grew more expensive and less regular, greater interest was shown in local food production, one result of which was the successful introduction of the bread-fruit tree from the Pacific.

The French islands, lacking a cheap reliable North American supplier, had always depended more than the British on locally grown food and had developed three systems of production which were also to be found in British territories. One of these was to cultivate part of the estate for food crops grown with plantation labor under plantation supervision. But the diversion of slave labor from sugar growing was never popular with the planters, and in the British territories this seems to have been seldom done except in emergency conditions. In some islands of both empires this system of food production seems to have been undertaken partly in response to laws enjoining on planters the raising of provisions when serious shortages, which might result in slave revolts or defensive weakness, were anticipated. A more common arrangement, even in such islands as Barbados, with very little land to spare from sugar, was to have small gardens adjacent to the Negro quarters, cultivated by the slaves in their spare time—normally a midday break, part of Saturday, and all of Sunday. The allocation of house plots had the advantage of raising some food without financial outlay or loss of working time on the part of the owner. Even if these garden plots did not succeed in feeding the plantation, they were believed to have a good effect on slave morale, as the industrious cultivator could dispose of his surplus produce and acquire small luxuries. In other territories with more space, such as Jamaica, a third system was found which made use on a much larger scale of the same technique of exploiting the slave's self-interest. Many estates contained hilly land not suitable for sugar but able to be made into substantial provision grounds on which slaves could raise a variety of tree, grain, and root crops, often adequate to feed themselves, with a surplus to be traded at the Sunday markets, which developed for the exchange of such produce. Reliance on local supplies was not, however, without dangers. A hurricane or, more often, a drought could affect crops and bring an area to starvation; and if supply ships were not normally required, and were not calling regularly, relief might be slow to organize. However food supplies were arranged, most of the planters seem to have devoted the minimum possible in cash or workers' time to them, and it is probable that most of the slave population hovered precariously around the level of bare subsistence. The great wealth of the West Indies applied only to the few fortunate among the planting class, and hunger as well as subjection was the lot of the great mass of the West Indian population in the age of slavery.

THE PLANTATION SOCIETY

The economics of slave-grown sugar had inexorable social consequences. Before the end of the seventeenth century African slave labor dominated the industry, and slaves were soon trained in the various crafts necessary for the running of a sugar estate, and came to be used as "drivers," or foremen, of field gangs. The requirement for Europeans in a plantation thus came to be restricted to a handful of managerial or supervisory personnel. Nor were opportunities much wider outside the sugar estates, for these dominated the economy. On some of the more populous islands there continued to be some employment for Europeans in mercantile and other urban pursuits, and in some islands small pockets of "poor whites" persisted, engaged in subsistence farming and somewhat isolated from the rest of the society; but even in these cases the proportion of Europeans to Africans tended to decline. This tendency was aided by the disinclination of many Europeans to settle permanently in the West Indies. The successful planter, especially from Jamaica and the British Leewards, often went to Europe and established himself in society there, living on the proceeds of his plantations, which he left in the hands of managers. Even those who stayed in the West Indies often sent their sons to Europe to be educated and their daughters to be married. Many from the planting class who left for Europe did not return to the Caribbean, and in this and other ways much property eventually came into the hands of people who had only an economic connection with the region and no commitment to West Indian society. The effect of these practices was cumulative. As more of the property owners came to reside in Europe, absentee ownership became more and more the general aspiration. The very paucity of numbers in the planting class made the islands socially unattractive for its members, and the absence of the most prosperous, the natural leaders of colonial society, made the development of a local community spirit and the provision of social amenities more difficult and less likely. Further down the social scale, whites employed as overseers or "bookkeepers" on estates, or in commerce, who were often recruited directly from the fortune-seekers, ne'er-do-wells or down-on-their-lucks of Europe, were perhaps even less likely to view their sojourn in the West Indies as permanent, even if in practice their prospects of getting rich quick and going home were rather slender. There was always a shortage of white women in the West Indies, and settled family life was infrequently achieved, especially by the poorly paid "bookkeeper." Moreover, the essentially rural nature of the economy and the self-contained structure of the individual plantation entailed the dispersal of the small white populations and militated against the development of coherent white communities. The only real restraint on complete white depopulation was the need to maintain control over the slaves.

This was a very genuine problem. The slaves in the sugar colonies had little prospect of any improvement in their situation, and it was far from unreasonable to suppose that they might resort to flight or to violence against their masters, especially, but not necessarily, if they were barbarous in their treatment of their slaves, as some were. Control could be facilitated through the creation of a relationship based on the masters' absolute power and superiority, and the slaves' absolute fear and subjection, and by the erection of a primitive social structure within the slave force of a particular estate, but in the last analysis the safety of the masters and the retention of their labor force depended on the slaves' expectation of punishment. The threat of mutilation or some particularly fearsome form of death was probably an adequate deterrent, if retribution appeared certain. But if the whites were few in number, or if concerted action among the slaves of even two or three neighboring estates could be organized, success might seem possible and the risk worth taking. Primitive communities of the descendants of runaways, among whom escaped slaves might take refuge, existed in various places. In Jamaica there were the settlements of Maroons (originally slaves of the Spaniards, who had taken to the hills when the British arrived), who caused much trouble until the government reached an agreement with them in 1739 that they should be left in peace, but return any fugitive slaves. In the Lesser Antilles runaways could try to make for unsubdued Carrib areas—in St. Vincent, for example, a community of "Black Caribs," said to have originated mainly from fugitive slaves from Barbados, grew up and was not brought under control until 1797, while in Surinam "Bush Negro" communities still exist in the forests of the interior. Loss of valuable property through escape was serious enough, but even more worrying was the danger to the planters' lives from slave revolts, a number of which occurred in most territories in the course of the eighteenth century, causing widespread apprehension until they were put down. If the slave's life was lived out in fear of the unbridled will of an unpredictable master, the master was constantly beset by fears of the terrible consequences of the revolt of slaves, who might combine the justified grievances of ill-used human beings with the primitive savagery of darkest Africa.

Such apprehensions were, no doubt, another factor reducing the attractiveness of the West Indies in the eyes of Europeans. At the same time, the need for slave control demanded the retention of at least a proportion of whites adequate to put down a slave revolt if one broke out, and, if possible, adequate to lead the slaves to believe that a rising was bound to fail. To this end the local assemblies in the British islands, which in general had smaller white proportions than the French, from time to time passed Deficiency Acts designed to force planters to maintain a certain ratio of white to slave employees. As white servants were difficult and expensive to come by, and as there was not much for them to do on the estates anyway, many planters began to find it cheaper to pay the fines than comply with the acts, which eventually became little more than revenue raising devices.

To some extent this problem was alleviated by another consequence of white depopulation, the emergence of a new category in the community which could share in the task of slave control, the free persons of color. Biologically, these groups resulted from the miscegenation which was promoted by the shortage of white women, and the absolute authority of the European owner or his employee over the slaves. White "bookkeepers," whose salaries could not support European wives, usually found a "housekeeper" from among the slave women. Although children of a slave mother inherited her legal status, the fathers often obtained the freedom of their slave offspring. In time such Europeans as could afford to do so took "housekeepers" from among the free colored women and proceeded to bring further free persons of color into the world. Before the end of slavery this group outnumbered the whites in many islands. Anxious above all to maintain their distinction from the slaves, they tried to identify themselves with the Europeans as far as they were permitted to do so by various legal and social disabilities. They were able, through service in the militia, to play a useful role in offsetting the dangerous predominance of the slaves, but not until the end of the eighteenth century were their numbers significant enough to moderate the rigid dichotomy of the society between management and labor, European and African, free and slave.

While white populations were tending to decline in the older colonies and were increasing only slowly even in the developing territories, slave populations everywhere in the sugar islands tended to increase in the eighteenth century. In the settled territories the increase was slow, necessitated largely by loss of soil fertility, which meant that more labor was required to cultivate the same amount of land. In the expanding colonies, such as Jamaica, slave population rose fast. These increases were due, for reasons already discussed, much more to immigration than to natural increase. There was thus an impermanence in the slave population even more marked than in the European population. There was also, among the slaves, much greater heterogeneity. Although a number of European powers contributed migrants to the West Indies, most of the inhabitants of any particular colony normally came from the same European country and shared much of a common culture, even though they might be from different classes of society. While it is difficult to be certain about the African origins of the West Indian slave populations (particularly as they were identified more by the port of shipment in Africa than by their area of origin, which might have been adjacent to the coast or several hundred miles inland), it is clear that the slaves came from agricultural, pastoral, and nomadic backgrounds, through capture in war, criminal condemnation, or simple kidnapping raids, and were shipped from various places along thousands of miles of the African coastline. Slaves from quite different parts of Africa were brought to the same colony in the same period, although there was a general tendency over time for the bulk of the trade to move east and south from its seventeenth-century centers in Senegambia and the Gold Coast toward Nigeria and Angola. Thus, although the majority of the slave force on a West Indian plantation would share an African background, this would seldom be a common African background. Some planters did show marked preferences for slaves of particular origins, but others deliberately refrained, for security purposes, from creating too homogeneous slave forces. While in some places the African heritage, particularly in religion and other non-material cultural elements, remained stronger than others, more significant everywhere was the pattern of adjustment to West Indian conditions, the "creolization" of the African immigrants. In this process the relatively smaller numbers of Creole slaves, those born in the West Indies, who had known no other environment than that of the plantation, were particularly significant. Both physically and psychologically the Creoles were better equipped to survive in West Indian conditions. They provided a much-needed element of continuity and generally filled many of the positions of responsibility on the plantations. Under their tutelage new slaves could be broken into plantation life, taught to communicate in Creole forms of European languages, and convinced of the uselessness of resistance to authority. Thus, long before the cessation of the slave trade, a form of slave society had begun to emerge on the plantation which made the slave community something more than an agglomeration of labor, and which mitigated some of the consequences of the evils inherent in a social system in which one group of human beings was the chattel possession of another.

COLONIAL POLITICS

The pattern of political as well as social life in the West Indies in the eighteenth century was largely determined by the domination of the sugar industry. Although executive government was in the hands of royal officials sent out from Europe, the planting interests had the advantage of greater permanence and local economic power, and were usually the decisive element in the local political scene. In the British islands they had an institutional mechanism for exerting their influence in the elected assemblies, representation in which was confined to white property owners. An assembly could coerce a governor by refusing to vote money for necessary expenditure until he approved any other measure the assembly was determined to pass. By giving in to such pressure the governor could involve himself in a violation of his instructions from London; but resistance could also lead to trouble, as the planters could use their influence in London to have a governor who was not amenable recalled. The home government expected the governor to uphold the Crown's rights and the ministry's policies, and in particular to raise adequate revenues to support colonial expenses, without coming into serious conflict with the assembly. As assemblies were reluctant to tax themselves, assertive of their constitutional rights and resentful of imperial dictation in local matters, this was a task calling for more political skill than most governors possessed. An able governor could try to maintain his position by exploiting the divisions which often existed within the assemblies (for example between planters and merchants, between different districts of the islands, or between greater and smaller proprietors). But most lacked the patience, the local knowledge, and the political acumen to manipulate the assemblies; and as a result conflict, often over the most trivial issues, was frequent. The governor, whose ambitions were centered in England rather than in the colonies, could not afford to alienate his ministerial patrons by capitulating to the assembly over any material point in his instructions. But the assembly, backed by local public opinion, had greater staying power than a governor who was isolated by thousands of miles from his source of authority, and in the long run it was the assembly that usually won. In general, the eighteenth century saw increased practical control by the local legislatures over the royal executives.

In the French colonies, although institutionally government was much more authoritarian (colonial assemblies only appearing at the end of the eighteenth century, and then without the power to initiate legislation), similar practical developments occurred with the increasing economic strength of the planters, whose ability to influence the conduct of government was considerable. In the course of the century the Dutch territories in Guiana also obtained local institutions in which the planters had some control over policy and finance.

As planter domination became securely established in the local political arena, the principal area of political conflict came to be between the colonies and the metropolitan governments. In the first half of the century differences were not too difficult to reconcile. In the age of European mercantilism, the economic importance of the colonies to the European powers was great. The West Indies, indeed, were almost the ideal mercantilist colonies. The use of slave labor meant that their exploitation did not denude the European country of manpower, and so weaken it in war. Sugar was essentially a non-European crop which did not compete with the mother country's production and which countries with colonies could sell at great profit to their less fortunate neighbors, once they had satisfied their domestic requirements. The concentration of the West Indies on sugar production, to the exclusion of almost all else, made the colonies an open market for manufactures and all manner of European exports; and their distance from Europe and their dependence on the slave trade demanded increased numbers of ships and seamen, who would also contribute to the naval security of the mother country. In such a climate of opinion it is not surprising that metropolitan policy was in general favorable to the planters' interests.

In the British territories there were, in the earlier part of the century, disputes over the question of local or metropolitan financial responsibility for defense. But the colonies were in a strong position, as they knew that Britain was not likely to allow matters to go to a point where there was a real risk of loss of the islands. The case of the Molasses Act of 1733 showed the willingness of the British government to put the interests of the West Indies before those of the North American mainland colonies. Here it could reasonably be represented that the interests of the British West Indies more or less coincided with those of the British Empire generally. But this coincidence diminished as costs of production rose, as sugar output failed to keep pace with increasing demand, and as the significance of the mainland colonies in the Empire increased. The West Indies, however, were able to push their own interests successfully with the British government for some time after these could no longer be regarded as identical with those of the Empire as a whole, largely through the development and organization of a powerful West Indian "lobby" in England. The creation of such a political "interest" in England was due mainly to the number and wealth of absentee owners, who resided in the mother country and were able to establish themselves in landed society and political influence. Some bought their way into the House of Commons and thus were able to make their influence felt directly on the legislature as well as indirectly through the executive. The planters found the growing body of West India factors and merchants in England, whose prosperity depended on that of their clients, in most cases their allies in furthering the West Indian cause; and by the 1760s the West India "interest" had reached the stage of organizing itself formally into bodies such as the Society of West India Planters and Merchants of London. The activities of this group probably had some influence on the decision to restore to France in 1763 such potentially dangerous competitors to the British islands as Guadeloupe and Martinique, and on the passing of the Sugar Act of 1764. This measure was designed to eliminate trading between the mainland colonies and the foreign West Indies, but its only important effect was to increase American resentment against the British authorities. From about this time the interests of the West India planters and those of the British Empire generally began to diverge further, and, although the West India "lobby" fought a stout rearguard action for primacy of esteem, it was unsuccessful in the long run—for example, in its attempt to continue trading with the United States after they no longer formed part of the British Empire.

If the first half of the century showed that there were limits on how far metropolitan authority could prudently be asserted in the British Caribbean, the second half showed that there were also limits to West Indian resistance to British authority. On the question of the constitutional relationship between colony and mother country, over issues such as the Stamp Act of 1765, the West Indians shared the viewpoint of the North American colonists. But they were unable to carry their objections to metropolitan policy to effective lengths, not only because the chances of successful armed resistance by small island colonies against a power with command of the sea could not be compared with the chance of the vast mainland colonies, but also because they were almost totally dependent on Britain for naval defense against foreign powers and, to a lesser extent, on British military forces for security against the dreadful possibility of slave revolt. This dependence was not only military but also economic, as, with rising costs, the British sugar islands had increasingly to rely on their protected position in the British market. As the eighteenth century went on the balance of political bargaining power tipped increasingly from the colonial to the metropolitan side.

The British situation was to a great extent reversed in the French islands in the late eighteenth century. Though the West India trade was a very important branch of French overseas commerce, France was less dependent than Britain on foreign trade. The West Indies were thus less vital to France, and metropolitan and Caribbean interests were more likely to diverge. Nor could such divergences be mitigated, as in England, by the political activities of a West Indian "lobby," for not only was the French political system less susceptible to this type of influence from such a source, but absentee ownership was less prevalent in the French territories, and there was much more of a conflict of interest between metropolitan merchants and colonial planters. The French merchants wished to control the French sugar market and the re-export trade to other parts of Europe as well as the supply and slave trades. But as French sugar production was competitive, the planter was not dependent on the metropolitan market and was in a position to make a better deal for himself by selling direct to the Dutch or other Europeans, and by buying his supplies from the Americans. From a position of such economic strength, and encouraged by the American example of successful colonial resistance to metropolitan authority, the French planters could try to agitate for a greater measure of self-government, and a freer trading system. But these possibilities had not long begun to emerge clearly before the whole situation, both metropolitan and local, was altered by the French Revolution of 1789 and the wars which followed it.

INTERNATIONAL RIVALRIES

Serious as they were, such political conflicts between colonies and their European mother countries were much less intense than the international rivalries between the metropolitan powers, which made war scarcely less normal than peace in the Caribbean in the age of slavery. As the importance of the sugar trade increased it became more and more the objective of European rivalry, in particular between Britain and France. But in the earlier years the riches of Spanish America continued to attract much attention, especially from the English. In the late seventeenth century Jamaica was valued quite as much for its possibilities as a base for trade, whether authorized or clandestine, with the Spanish colonies, as for its sugar-producing potential. The most obvious way of breaking the closely guarded monopoly of the Spanish empire was through the trade in slaves, always in short supply and in brisk demand in the Spanish colonies. Spain had never been able to supply her own requirements from Africa, and it had become her practice to make a contract, or *asiento*, usually with the Portuguese, for supplies of slaves. Spain's stipulations about quality and price were often difficult to fulfill, the arrangements seldom in fact proved profitable to the participants, and the system broke down completely during the Dutch domination of the Caribbean in the middle of the seventeenth century. But the belief persisted that the *asiento* was a valuable concession and that the possession of it might open the way for more general trading privileges in the Spanish empire. The English soon became interested in the *asiento*, when, in the 1660s, a newly licensed partnership of Genoese concessionaires began to purchase the slaves, which they contracted to supply, in the British West Indies, and Spanish ships began to visit British Caribbean ports, with special permission, for the purpose of picking up slaves. There was opposition to this from the planters, who also needed the slaves and found that competition with the Spanish market forced up prices and left them with inadequate supplies of poorer quality. But the bullion which this foreign slave trade brought in was most welcome, and the contacts thus established encouraged the development of an unofficial trade in commodities as well; and, on the whole, at this time the slavers got more support from the British government than the planters. Spain, however, declined to change her general attitude to her colonial monopoly and British attempts to negotiate an *asiento* in the late seventeenth century were not successful.

Where the British failed, the French, who had also shown an increasing interest in Spanish America and the *asiento*, succeeded, when the royal Hapsburg line of Spain died out in 1700 and the throne passed to the Bourbon candidate, a grandson of the French king. The assignment of the *asiento* to a French company soon afterward was one of a number of indications of the danger to England of close Franco-Spanish cooperation, which led to Britain's participation in the War of Spanish Succession in an attempt to unseat the Bourbon King of Spain. Although this objective was not realized, Britain was successful enough in the war to demand not only various safeguards for herself and her allies, but also the *asiento* (which the war had prevented the French from exercising), coupled with the novel concession of one ship a year to trade in merchandise with the Spanish colonies.

Even on paper these privileges were a good deal less than had been hoped for, and in practice they turned out to be thoroughly disappointing. The *asiento*, as always, proved hard to comply with, and the trade of the annual ship, restricted to the single port of Puerto Bello after the arrival of the supply fleet from Spain, was found to be of so little value that the right was exercised only eight times in over thirty years. Moreover, the existence of these limited concessions, which were assigned to a single English concern, the South Sea Company (which naturally became opposed to the intervention of other English traders), was believed to have worsened the position of English merchants trading both legally with the Spanish colonies through Spain, in partnership with Spanish firms, and illegally directly with Spanish America from the Caribbean. Unable any longer to control the seaways of the Caribbean, the Spaniards sought to preserve their monopoly by licensing private individuals as *guardacostas* to act against illegal traders. As the *guardacostas* were paid by results, from a share of the proceeds of condemned prizes, they were not too careful in discriminating between legal and illegal trading by other nations, and the local Spanish courts usually accepted the presence on board of certain types of commodity (even though these were produced in foreign as well as Spanish colonies) or of Spanish coins (even though these circulated freely all around the Caribbean) as evidence of illegal trade. Thus many English ships trading legally within the bounds of the British Empire were seized, as well as ships trading clandestinely with Spanish America. This "buccaneering in reverse" inflamed local feelings and aroused the ire of the West India "interest" to such a pitch that not even a successful negotiation with the Spanish metropolitan government could avert the outbreak of an Anglo-Spanish war in 1739, and after its conclusion the *asiento* and annual ship arrangements were abandoned. Clandestine trade continued, though the reorganization of the Spanish Empire in the 1760s and 1770s had the effect of reducing its importance. This and other grievances, such as the British logwood-cutting establishments in the Bay of Honduras, brought Spain into the Seven Years War and the American Revolutionary War against Britain. But already in the 1740s the merging of the Anglo-Spanish into an Anglo-French war had demonstrated a shift in the main focus of Caribbean rivalry.

In the series of Anglo-French wars between the 1740s and the 1780s the main concern was trade rather than conquest. Although a number of islands did change hands, such acquisitions were not the most important objectives, though they were sometimes the only noticeable consequences, of the Caribbean campaigns. The prime issue at stake in these wars in the West Indies was the British sugar trade which was of great importance in the British economy and the loss of which was likely to impair Britain's capacity to fight European or colonial wars. By contrast, the French trade was less vital to France. Britain's highest priority therefore was defense, and France's attack, and this determined the very different strategic approaches of the two countries in the Caribbean. The most economical form of French attack was by privateers, operating both from the French West Indies and from France itself in the western approaches to England. To counter these dangers, the British organized convoys and established naval stations in the West Indies, where they permanently maintained small forces of warships to protect the trade and operate against privateers. At times the French were more ambitious, and fitted out large-scale expeditions in France to sail to the West Indies and attack British islands. Such schemes were always potentially dangerous to the British, for any large expedition could outclass the small British squadrons, which normally enjoyed local naval superiority. Even temporary control of British islands could be devastating, as the sugar industry could be ruined for years by the carrying off of its most vital form of capital, the slave force (though in practice a prompt capitulation to the enemy by the planters of either side at the first threat usually sufficed to save their estates from destruction). But great expeditions from France were infrequent and seldom successful. Britain was usually able to blockade French ports. If a French fleet did escape, the British would send naval reinforcements to the West Indies that could meet the French on more or less equal terms. Lacking West Indian bases, the French expedition had only a limited time to strike a blow before it had to return home. Above all, it usually had to put in at the French islands to reorganize and take on provisions after the Atlantic crossing before launching any attack, and immediately losses from disease among the troops would begin to mount—malaria, dysentery, and yellow fever being the greatest hazards in any Caribbean campaign by forces from Europe. Only in the American Revolutionary War, when Britain's naval power was seriously overextended, did the French achieve much in the Caribbean.

Though less vital than defense, attacking French trade was, of course, also an important British object. Indeed, so great was the danger of British capture that trade between France and her West Indian colonies was often brought virtually to a standstill in wartime. This, however, did not harm the French islands as much as it might have done, as the British North American colonists found the profit to be obtained from supplying the French islands with provisions, which became even greater in war than in peace, too great a temptation for their patriotism to resist; and the Dutch were always willing to carry French sugar to Europe under their neutral flag. The wars of the eighteenth century made of the tiny Dutch island of St. Eustatius a great free port resorted to by all and sundry until the British, provoked by the large-scale Dutch supply of the American revolutionaries, declared war and captured it, along with 150 ships engaged in contraband trade and enormous quantities of goods, in 1781. In the Seven Years War the British, too, sent expeditions to the West Indies, which took a number of islands from the French. Britain's motives, however, were much more strategic and diplomatic than economic. St. Lucia was captured to enable the British to keep an eye on the French privateers of neighboring Martinique. Guadeloupe and Martinique were taken somewhat later to be used as pawns at the conference table in exchange for British territories lost in other parts of the world. They were allowed to capitulate on favorable terms and were returned, along with St. Lucia, at the end of the war, when only the less important French islands were retained by Britain. In much the same way, most of the British islands captured by the French in the American Revolutionary war were returned at the peace. This last was much the most serious conflict for the British islands, for not only did the French often have naval superiority, but the British were also at war with their normal suppliers, the North Americans, and some islands experienced famine, and all, high prices and costs. On the whole, however, neither the British nor the French sugar industry was permanently impaired by the campaigning or by the disruptions of trade; in fact, in the two earlier wars, the British planters seem to have profited considerably from the emergency conditions.

Considering how much was attempted in the Caribbean, the wars of the eighteenth century had remarkably little result. Disease of course always hampered campaigning; but the venality on the part of commanders and officials, which prevented the pressing home of advantages, and the widespread smuggling and contraband, which mitigated the rigors of blockade, were symptomatic of a lack of enthusiasm among the colonists for wars that were often felt to be European rather than Caribbean affairs. The islanders naturally tended to think rather provincially than imperially, and their reactions are understandable. Though Caribbean events sometimes had a contributory effect on European diplomacy and decisions on war or peace, this was seldom decisive, for, from the point of view of the British and the French, the Caribbean was only one of many theaters of war in a long struggle which did not reach a decisive outcome until 1815.

During the last years of the eighteenth century and the first half of the nineteenth the West Indian situation was completely transformed. On the international level, Britain emerged from the French Revolutionary and Napoleonic Wars with a strategic predominance which lasted until the beginning of the twentieth century. Paradoxically, however, this supremacy was achieved just at the time when changes in the British economy were occurring which made it much less of an advantage than it would have been even half a century earlier. The emphasis of the British economy was shifting from commerce to manufacturing industry, and the call was for free world trade in place of exclusive imperial systems. In such a context the high-cost British sugar islands were no longer assured of privileged treatment, and from being an important element in a commercial empire they became an almost superfluous adjunct to the "workshop of the world." This loss of economic significance assisted, in fact was probably a precondition of, the success of the humanitarian agitation against slavery, which had originated quite independently. Effective first in the British territories, but later extending to the rest of the area, the campaign to end slavery added fundamental social change to the changes already in train in the economic and political spheres.

COCKPIT TO BACKWATER

International rivalry in the Caribbean was still intense when war broke out in 1793 between England and revolutionary France. Both sides still saw the Caribbean as an important theater of war, and a considerable part of the British effort was made there. In 1793 Tobago was captured from the French, and in 1794 the British were also successful in taking Martinique, St. Lucia, and Guadeloupe, assisted to some extent by French royalist planters opposed to the

republican government of France. A revolutionary force sent out
from France, however, recaptured Guadeloupe some months later,
retook St. Lucia in the next year, and stirred up internal revolts
among the surviving French planters in the British colonies of Dominica, Grenada, and St. Vincent, which were not quelled until the
arrival of a new British expedition in 1796, which also brought St.
Lucia once again under British control. By this time the Netherlands
had fallen under French rule and entered the war on France's side,
and Spain, unsuccessful in war against France from 1793, had
changed sides and allied with the French against the British, who
proceeded to act against the Caribbean colonies of these powers.
The Dutch colonies in Guiana were occupied from 1796, and the
Dutch Antilles in 1800 and 1801, and, although an English attack
on Puerto Rico in 1797 had been unsuccessful, Spain had earlier in
the year lost Trinidad, regarded by Britain as of particular importance, both because of the threat to British-held territories from the
substantial French population recently settled there under the new
Spanish immigration policy, and because of its convenient situation
for further activities against Spanish America. Though the British
added to their conquests the Danish Virgin Islands and Swedish St.
Barthélemy in 1801, in the peace at the end of that year only Trinidad was retained. The resumption of war in 1803, again involving
a number of other European countries on France's side, led, especially after the securing of British naval supremacy at Trafalgar in
1805, to British occupation this time of all Dutch, French, and Danish territories in the West Indies by 1810. But of these conquests
only St. Lucia, Tobago, and the three Dutch colonies that were later
amalgamated into British Guiana became permanently British at
the peace of 1815.

While British holdings were substantially increased in this period
at the expense of the other powers, of much greater ultimate significance were the other losses suffered in the area by France and Spain.
The first of these was Saint-Domingue. The French Revolution of
1789 led to metropolitan vacillations and local quarrels erupting into
sporadic civil war over the demands of whites and free people of
color, in the midst of which a slave rebellion broke out in 1791. The
worst fears of eighteenth-century planters came true as whites were
massacred and plantations destroyed. Local resources were inadequate to suppress the rising, and when reinforcements came from
republican France these took the part of the slaves against the royal-
ist-inclined planters and decreed their emancipation. The planters

enlisted English support, and from 1793 British forces attempted unsuccessfully to capture what had been the most valuable colony in the West Indies. In 1798 they gave up the unequal battle against the ravages of disease and the skill of the ex-slave general Toussaint L'Ouverture, who emerged in effective control of the French colony. When the European war ended temporarily in 1801, a strong French force was despatched to bring Saint-Domingue again under metropolitan control, with the probable intention of re-establishing slavery; but it was resisted by the Negro forces and soon began to succumb to yellow fever. With the resumption of war against Britain in 1803, the French in Saint-Domingue, cut off by British sea power, were doomed. They soon surrendered to the blockading squadrons, leaving the new Negro masters of the territory to establish the independent state of Haiti. The sale of Louisiana to the United States at the same time was indicative of Napoleon's loss of interest in the Americas. At the end of the war, with Saint-Domingue irretrievably lost (planter hopes of recovery finally being dashed when French rights were officially abandoned in the 1820s), and her possessions reduced to Guadeloupe, Martinique, and French Guiana, France had no basis for re-emergence as a Caribbean power.

Even more cataclysmic was the eclipse of Spain. Colonial resentment against the mother country had for some time been growing in the Spanish colonies, and the impulse toward self-government was given further impetus by the virtual cutting off of imperial communications during the wars of 1796-1801 and 1804-08 against England. During this period the British considered various schemes for stimulating, or assisting with military force, an independence movement in the colonies, and the promotion of such projects was one of the reasons for the acquisition of Trinidad. When, however, the Napoleonic invasion of Spain and deposition of its royal house turned Spain from enemy to ally, Britain's policy naturally altered, but these events gave a further boost to the independence movement in the Spanish colonies, which finally prevailed, after a lengthy struggle against both local loyalists and Spanish troops. In the early 1820s Spain emerged with only Cuba and Puerto Rico still in her hands, having lost her vast possessions in Mexico and Central and South America. The opening of these former Spanish colonies to direct trade with Europe and the virtual impossibility of the effective re-establishment by other European powers of a position in the Caribbean at all comparable to that which the British had won deprived the area of the great strategic significance it had assumed in earlier years and rendered it no longer a matter of European diplomatic or military significance, as the imperial activities of European powers were more and more directed to other parts of the world.

PROSPERITY TO DEPRESSION

Effective British dominance might not have gone so long unchallenged had not the economic as well as the strategic importance of the region undergone a marked decline at this time. This was at first relative, rather than absolute, and stemmed from the great expansion of the economy and of the population of Europe, and particularly of England, which took place from the late eighteenth century. Although sugar production did increase—especially in the relatively low-cost newer producers, Trinidad, Puerto Rico, and British Guiana, and even, under stimulus of war and the complete loss of Saint-Domingue's production, in some of the older ones—the West Indian trade formed a less and less important element in the overseas commerce of European powers. This was outstandingly so in the case of Britain, despite her acquisitions of West Indian territory, for the "industrial revolution" was leading to an enormous expansion of exports of manufactured goods, and sugar was beginning to be seen less as a valuable commercial commodity than as a necessary foodstuff which should be kept as cheap as possible so that living costs, and therefore wages, costs of production, and prices of manufactures could be kept down to ensure a competitive position in export markets. During the wars Britain's conquest of most of the producing territories, coupled with the cessation of production in Saint-Domingue, had given her a virtual monopoly, and, despite occasional gluts of the European market, prices had remained fairly high. But thereafter new areas with much larger capacities for expansion were coming into production on an unprecedented scale in places such as Cuba, Brazil, and the East Indies, capturing the world markets, and forcing down prices below the level at which the planters in the older British colonies could make a satisfactory profit. For some time their position in the British market was protected by preferential import duties, but from the start these did not operate against the newly acquired West Indian colonies, and British Guiana in particular increased its share of the British market until in the late 1830s it equaled that of Jamaica. Further competition came from Mauritius (a colony acquired from the French in the Napoleonic wars) and British India, both of which were by the 1840s producing quantities similar to Jamaica, after the import duties on their sugar had been reduced to the same level as that on West Indian sugar in 1825 and 1836 respectively. When finally, after progressive reductions of the differential in the 1840s, foreign-grown sugar was admitted to Britain from 1854 at the same rate of duty as colonial, production in many British territories became economic only for the most efficient producers. Although the basic problem facing the planters was one of world markets and sources of supply over which they could have little control, they were at least in part responsible for their own plight. By the end of the eighteenth century signs of inefficiency were already apparent in the industry, but in general the planters, instead of trying to improve their economic performance and make their production competitive on the world market, sought rather to maintain their position by political action, which, with the general movement toward free trade, succeeded only in delaying the need to face economic realities; and when the day of reckoning came, many went under.

So heavily were the British West Indies committed to the single activity of sugar production that other effects of the "industrial revolution," such as the stimulation of West Indian cotton production and the establishment of Free Ports in the West Indies to expand trade with foreign colonies, gave little relief. These measures were, in any case, only of significance in the earlier stages of the economic changes when the concept of an exclusive, or at least a preferential, imperial system had not been abandoned in favor of free trade. Between about 1790 and 1810 there was a considerable expansion of West Indian cotton exports, but thereafter enormously expanded supplies from the southern United States soon took over the British market. Similarly, the Free Port system, first set up in 1766 with the primary intention of increasing the sale of slaves to the Spanish colonies by admitting their ships and produce to certain colonial ports, and later expanded in the hope of increasing the market for British manufactures, might have been expected to bring some prosperity from the development of the West Indies as an entrepot for commerce. But the independence of Spanish America soon led to the opening up of direct trade with Europe and made the use of West Indian ports largely unnecessary. Such increases as took place in the commercial significance of the West Indies as a result of expanded European trade in the Caribbean area could by no means offset the economic effects of the adverse developments in the British sugar market.

These, of course, were particularly marked in Jamaica, Barbados, and the Leewards. Trinidad, the Guianas, and Puerto Rico were, in the period following the Napoleonic wars, only starting large-scale sugar production, and in Puerto Rico considerable assistance was given by the Spanish government. In the French islands, too, protection continued and production revived and rose to much higher levels than before the wars. But new difficulties were already emerging with the rise of the metropolitan beet-sugar industry, which was stimulated during the blockades of the Napoleonic Wars, continued to receive governmental assistance, and, by the 1830s, was producing one-third of French domestic sugar consumption. The increased sugar output of the Lesser Antilles and the Guianas was, however, dwarfed by the great growth of production in Cuba and territories outside the Caribbean area. By the middle of the nineteenth century the economy of the West Indian islands had been left far behind by sensational developments in various fields in many other parts of the world.

SLAVERY TO FREEDOM

The depression which hit the West Indies in the nineteenth century was undoubtedly worsened by what was, in the long run, the most important change of all, the ending of slavery. Not unnaturally, planters tended to blame this fundamental alteration in their system of production, forced on them by metropolitan action, for all their difficulties; and, although these were really of wider and deeper origin, the economic and social changes were not unrelated. In the first place, it is clear that slave emancipation did not begin to be seriously contemplated in influential circles until the reorientation of the needs of European economies had greatly reduced the significance of West Indian sugar production. But it is more difficult to demonstrate that metropolitan economic changes positively necessitated the destruction of the slave system. Though competing economic interests were to be found among the opponents and defenders of West Indian slavery, the drive for emancipation came primarily from "humanitarians" who were convinced that slavery was an evil, and the success of this campaign, particularly in Britain, came primarily from the changed economic circumstances which made it possible for the British to act on moral grounds without significant material sacrifice.

In Britain humanitarian agitation was directed first against the slave trade rather than against the institution of slavery itself, and a campaign was carried on persistently in Parliament from the late

1780s. The only early success was a minor one—an act of 1790 limiting the number of slaves that could be packed into a vessel. But the fact that the degree of discomfort or danger to which slaves should be subjected had become matter for public attention indicated some shift in attitudes. Indeed, both planters and abolitionists saw the antislave-trade agitation as only the thin end of the wedge. The humanitarians hoped that the cutting off of fresh supplies from Africa would force the planters to conserve their slave forces more carefully, exploit them less ruthlessly, and generally create conditions under which their natural increase would become possible, as well as put a stop to what was an evil in itself. After slave conditions had been ameliorated under stress of such necessity, it was felt that the gradual transition from slavery to freedom would not be difficult. The planters pointed out that if Britain outlawed the trade unilaterally, the chief beneficiaries would be the French, whose system of production would not suffer disruption; but the abolitionists hoped for international action and were encouraged by the actions of like-minded groups in France, such as the Société des Amis des Noirs, though some French interests construed English abolitionism as a perfidious move by the less successful sugar empire to cripple the more successful.

In the event, the ascendancy of the extremist democratic wing in the French Revolution led to the precipitate abolition of slavery itself in 1794. The only colony in which this took effect (apart from Saint-Domingue, events in which have already been noted) was Guadeloupe, which was under revolutionary control for a few years, and in 1802 slavery was restored by Napoleon. The excesses of the French Revolution and the exigencies of war meant that reform proposals got little hearing in England for some years, but the campaign for abolition of the slave trade was never entirely abandoned and gained ground again around 1804, amidst somewhat lessening opposition. The planters in the old West Indian colonies were a little less averse to abolition, for they felt that it could be expected to delay the emergence of serious competition from Trinidad and British Guiana (which, though not annexed until 1815, had been in British hands with only a short break from 1796). Further, the dependence of British ports such as Liverpool on the slave trade had much declined since the 1780s, as new opportunities opened for their shipping. In 1807 an act got through making it an offence for British subjects or ships to engage in slave trading.

The abolitionist agitation did not end there; it was next carried abroad with a view to the entire suppression of the trade from Africa by persuading other nations to ban it, and in this international campaign the abolitionists could usually hope to enjoy the support of some British economic interests, concerned with stopping for everyone an activity in which they could not participate. Denmark and the United States had already taken action to stop their nationals trading in slaves, and, at the end of the Napoleonic wars, the other major Atlantic slave traders—France, the Netherlands, Spain, and Portugal—entered into antislave-trade treaties with Britain, though the Iberian powers especially were much less rigorous than the British in enforcing laws against the trade, which continued to flourish in several areas for many years. Of the territories covered by this study, however, none received very significant numbers of slaves from Africa after the end of the Napoleonic wars.

The British humanitarians had hoped that the abolition of the slave trade of itself would tend to improve slave conditions in the West Indies, but the results did not come up to their expectations. Within a few years some were already convinced that more direct action to promote the amelioration of slavery would be necessary, and by 1823 the Anti-Slavery Society had been formed to take the matter up seriously in Parliament and the country generally. Action directed toward amelioration or emancipation was, for constitutional reasons, more difficult than action against the slave trade. Imperial trade and shipping were within the undoubted province of the metropolitan Parliament, but laws relating to slavery were a matter for colonial legislatures. Although in theory these could be overridden by acts of the British Parliament, the constitutional disputes with the North American colonies, which had led on to revolution and independence, seemed to suggest that the exercise of supreme legislative power by Britain would be a course of action of the most doubtful wisdom. The problem facing the humanitarians, therefore, was to induce the colonial assemblies, which were dominated by the slave-owners, to enact laws to humanize the institution in which they were vitally interested. This difficulty did not, however, apply in all the British West Indian territories. The Windward Islands, acquired in 1763, were the last to which representative assemblies of the old type were granted by the Crown. In a subsequent legal case it was ruled that establishment of such institutions deprived the Crown of all future right to exercise lawmaking or taxing powers, and so, in the formulation of later colonial constitutions, care was taken by the British executive to retain such rights in its own hands. A further factor operating in the same direction was the growing conviction that the precipitate introduction of British laws and institutions into territories annexed from other European powers, and containing largely non-British populations, was inadvisable; and so, in the territories occupied or acquired during the Napoleonic Wars, much of the legal and constitutional *status quo* was preserved, despite objections from British settlers that they were entitled to the rights and liberties of British subjects. In the cases of British Guiana, Trinidad, and St. Lucia, therefore, it was possible for the British Colonial Office, without resort to Parliamentary enactments, to initiate laws in a way that it could not do for the other territories.

Under humanitarian influence, the Colonial Office and the Cabinet became prepared to adopt an amelioration policy which involved such reforms in slave codes as restriction of physical punishment, prohibition of the separate sale of parents and children, admissibility of slave evidence in courts of law, and encouragement of Christian marriage among slaves. These became law for Trinidad, St. Lucia and British Guiana, where the British Government had retained authority, and the Colonial Office requested the governors of the colonies with assemblies to urge these to pass similar legislation. This these bodies refused to do, with the exception of a few minor enactments, interpreted in Britain as empty gestures intended to try to avert further metropolitan interference. Even where ameliorative laws were passed, the extent of their effect was probably slight, as it was from the white slave-owning classes that the colonial law-enforcement agencies and judicial authorities were drawn.

Although the campaign of the humanitarians in England for amelioration thus suffered from constitutional and practical limitations, the missionary wing of the movement had for some years been engaged in the West Indies on what many thought the most important means of slave improvement, Christian religious instruction. Although European colonists had carried their Christianity with them to the West Indies, and in the French and Spanish colonies Catholic orthodoxy had been officially upheld and supported by government, in general Christianity remained the religion of Europeans only. French metropolitan regulations enjoined the conversion of the slaves, but there were never enough clergy to implement this policy, which was in any case strongly opposed by most planters throughout the region. Although they did not believe that Christianity was incompatible with slave-owning, they did feel that the instruction of the slaves in its doctrines would be dangerous, as tending to undermine the basis of white ascendancy as supposedly superior beings. The clergy were often prevented by the planters from undertaking missionary work among their slaves, and most seem to have conformed without many qualms to the views of the society. Toward the end of the eighteenth century, however, the same intellectual climate as produced the humanitarian movement in England gave rise to an evangelical movement which both operated inside the established Church of England and led to the development of vigorous nonconformist churches, such as the Methodist and the Baptist. Evangelical activity was not confined to Britain, and from the late eighteenth century, and increasingly after 1815, missionaries were sent to preach among the slaves of the West Indies. Despite obstruction from the planters and the obvious difficulties of working in untutored communities whose time was not their own, the missionaries appear to have made a substantial impact on at least some parts of the slave populations, if only by relieving to some extent their almost total ignorance of anything outside the immediate plantation environment, both directly and by instruction in reading. Although the parent missionary societies instructed their ministers carefully to avoid any teaching against slavery, or the creation of any dissatisfaction among the slaves with their status, there was inherent conflict between the general concept of the Christian brotherhood, and such detailed precepts as Sabbath observance, and the slave's subordination to his master and his need to work when he was told. The very activity of the missionaries appears to have suggested to the slaves that people in England were evincing an interest of an entirely new sort in them, and looking on them as other than mere beasts of burden. Ideas of freedom began to be very much in the air around the plantations. The slaves became more restive, and risings, often based on a belief that freedom had been granted by the authorities but withheld by their owners, became more frequent. For these troubles the planters blamed the activities of the missionaries, and in a notorious case in British Guiana in the 1820s a missionary was condemned to death for his supposed connection with a slave revolt. In other territories colonists, enraged by slave risings, burned down missionary chapels and threatened the lives of preachers. Although in fact missionaries seem to have tried to restrain their congregations from joining in rebellious acts, the wrath of the planters was not entirely misdirected. The presence of missionaries, whose sympathies plainly lay with the slaves rather than the planters, undoubtedly intensified the perennial problem of slave control.

The increased difficulties with the slaves, combined with the threat of the antislavery movement in England, contributed to an important local development of this time, the improvement of the position of free persons of color who, at the end of the eighteenth century, still suffered from a number of legal and social disabilities. But they were increasing in numbers and in wealth. Discouraged from large-scale landowning, many went into mercantile business and prospered during the trade expansion of the Napoleonic wars to such an extent that they were able to buy out planters who were hit by the postwar depression in sugar. A great number of the free colored were slave-owners on a small scale, and thus their interests in the slavery issue were likely to be similar to those of the Europeans. They had already succeeded in having a number of discriminatory laws against them removed when, in the late 1820s, the whites in some territories began to think it might be advisable to range them firmly on their side against the threat of Negro freedom. In the next few years color-based legal distinctions between free men were largely removed in the British territories, basically with a view to strengthening the ruling classes by admitting new categories to them.

Such a broader basis of local resistance to the antislavery movement was, however, to be of no avail. The general refusal of the colonial assemblies to adopt the amelioration measures urged on them by the Colonial Office gravely weakened their case for retaining the institution of slavery in the eyes of a British Parliament and public which the Anti-Slavery Society's efficient propaganda machine had bombarded with genuine, if perhaps exceptional, horror stories of slave conditions. Possibly even more damaging to the planters was the effect produced among the increasingly influential evangelical circles in England by their treatment of missionaries in the West Indies. Refusal to be dictated to by the Colonial Office was one thing; direct and violent action against the spread of Christianity among the slaves was quite another, and appeared to indicate that the West Indian ruling classes were not so much concerned with the preservation of their colonial constitutional rights as they were determined by any means to resist any improvement in the condition of their slaves. In these circumstances the Anti-Slavery Society abandoned its policy of promoting amelioration as a means to the gradual elimination of slavery, and in 1830 came out in favor of immediate complete emancipation.

Political circumstances in Britain were favorable. In 1830 the movement for the reform of the British Parliament came to a head and brought into power a ministry more firmly committed to liberal reforming measures. Its first important success was the passing of the Reform Act of 1832, which extended the franchise to the new industrial middle classes, and abolished or enlarged a number of the constituencies which had become the virtual personal possessions of individuals. Not only did this reduce the direct representation of the West India interest in the House of Commons, but it marked the success of a campaign, one of the important elements in which was the stressing of personal as against property rights. The upholders of the unreformed Parliamentary system had tended to regard the vote, and in some cases the constituency, as a species of property, and had resisted reform as an attack on the sanctity of property. Their defeat made psychologically easier the invasion of another form of property right, that of the proprietor in his slaves, which was involved in the Slave Emancipation Act which became law in 1833 in the first Parliament elected under the new arrangements. On the fundamental point of the legal status of the slaves, the Act was uncompromising, but it did make some concessions to the planters' position. In the first place, the transition to freedom was to be eased by a period of four to six years of "apprenticeship," during which most freed slaves would have to spend most of the working week in the employment of their former masters; and, in the second place, the Act provided for financial compensation for the loss of property by voting £20,000,000 from the British Treasury to be paid to the slave owners, of which sum four-fifths was disbursed in respect of slaves in the West Indies. These aspects of the British act of emancipation to some extent sugared the pill and induced the planters to give up the struggle. The constitutional issue was circumvented by leaving the local implementation of emancipation to the legislation of the colonial assemblies, and their cooperation, which had been so noticeably lacking over amelioration, was ensured by providing that only in colonies that passed satisfactory emancipation measures would the compensation money be made available.

Perhaps as important in securing the planters' acquiescence in emancipation as the prospect of some compensation and at least a few years of guaranteed labor supply, was the growing difficulty of slave control. In Jamaica there was a serious slave rising at the end of 1831, and throughout the British territories the slaves had come to believe that freedom was imminent. Distasteful as emancipation was to the planters, they could hope to salvage something from a compensated orderly emancipation, and if the prospects before them seemed gloomy they were at least preferable to a repetition of Saint-Domingue.

Emancipation in the French colonies followed fifteen years later, after a somewhat similar sequence of events. Metropolitan pressure for amelioration had been more successful, due to the lack of local assemblies in the colonies which could form a focus of opposition; in particular, the right conceded to the slaves of compulsory manumission was widely exercised and greatly reduced the proportion of the population still to be freed in 1848. The same year saw the slaves freed in the Danish islands, after they had revolted in resistance to a scheme for gradual emancipation; and in 1863 emancipation took effect in the Dutch colonies. In Puerto Rico, however, the emancipation in 1873 of the very much smaller percentage of the population held in slavery was the result of several years of local pressure on a Spanish metropolitan government reluctant to take action for fear of repercussions in its other Caribbean colony, Cuba, then involved in civil war. Emancipation was thus not completed in all the territories under consideration for four decades after the British act. However, far more people were affected in the British colonies than in all the others together, and the social and economic changes involved in these territories were of very great significance. In a very real sense it can be said that the 1830s inaugurated a new phase in the history of the West Indian islands.

FIVE

DEPENDENCE AND STAGNATION

Emancipation was clearly a precondition of any real social progress for the slaves but, though it was certainly enthusiastically welcomed by those it freed, emancipation in itself could not guarantee that progress would be realized. In fact, for a century after the British emancipation it was extremely slow. In part this was due to economic weaknesses attributable much less to the abolition of slavery than to various external factors, and the long persistence of a stagnant economy was in turn due to a great extent to continued political dependence on metropolitan countries whose prevalent economic philosophies were ill-adapted to coping with the problems of colonial depression. Yet freedom did bring about substantial social change, especially in immensely widening the area of choice for the mass of the population. Very many, in fact, chose not to continue working on the sugar plantations. This withdrawal of labor not only raised economic difficulties for the sugar industry, but had profound social implications. The general response of the ex-slave populations, wherever practicable, was to repudiate the sugar estate as a way of life. The meaning of freedom was essentially the ending of the tyranny of the plantation.

POST-EMANCIPATION SOCIETY

Despite attempts in most of the British territories, later followed by somewhat similar arrangements in some of the Dutch, to habituate ex-slaves to the idea of continuing to work for wages on the plantation by a compulsory apprenticeship system under which, for the first few years of freedom, they were obliged to spend some three-quarters of the working week in the employment of their former masters, the reaction against plantation work when full freedom came was very general. The form it took, however, naturally varied according to local conditions. In Jamaica, the French islands, and the mountainous Windwards there were hill areas unsuitable for sugar cultivation or marginal sugar areas cultivated in earlier boom-times but no longer economic in the mid-nineteenth century, on which ex-slaves could establish small holdings. In Trinidad and the Guianas, where cultivation had not reached its limits, land was also available for settlement. In these territories many ex-slaves were able to become completely independent farmers, and many more semi-independent, only occasionally seeking wage work on the plantations. On the other hand, in such fully exploited islands as Barbados and Antigua there was no room for the emergence of an independent peasantry. Emigration, however, was a possibility in such cases, either to territories with some land available, or, more commonly, either seasonally or permanently to Trinidad, or even British Guiana, where shortage of labor made for high wage rates. One interesting example of post-emancipation emigration is that of ex-slaves from the Cayman Islands to the virtually uninhabited Bay Islands off the coast of Honduras (made a British colony for a short time in the 1850s), where they raised fruit for the New Orleans market.

In an atmosphere where the ex-slave felt his new-found dignity as a free man impaired by estate labor, it is doubtful whether anything the planters could have done in the way of making pay and conditions more attractive could have retained their labor force. In fact, of course, most of them did not try, as planter attitudes to ex-slaves on the whole changed no more with emancipation than did ex-slave attitudes to planters, and coercion rather than attraction was the technique adopted to get workers. Planters tried to make tenancy of house plots contingent on regular estate labor or to bind workers to them in labor contracts, and, through their continued influence on legislation, they were able to impose taxes which would tend to make wage work necessary, to put difficulties in the way of acquiring land, and to attempt to restrain emigration. Such measures only served to heighten the determination of the Negro population to avoid estate work if possible, and in several islands the labor problem was a major contributory factor in the collapse of a sugar industry already facing many difficulties. In many territories the planters soon realized that the labor of ex-slaves was going to be too intermittent and costly for the profitable operation of sugar estates, and they looked to a new inflow of workers from outside the area to force down wage rates in older territories and enable expansion to take place in newer ones.

The net was cast wide. Some Negro slaves liberated from captured slave ships were obtained, but the numbers were small. Europeans and Africans were, in general, difficult to recruit. Portuguese from Madeira came in large numbers, but soon deserted agriculture for business, as did most Chinese immigrants. Much the most important source of immigrants came to be India. After a few false starts a regular traffic was established by about 1850, controlled and supervised by the governments concerned, to bring Indian workers as indentured laborers to the West Indies. Over half-a-million came in this way until the Indian Government stopped the practice in 1917. These East Indian immigrants were normally contracted to work on a sugar estate for a period of five years, after which, at first, they were entitled to a passage home. Later this was made available only after ten years, and still later only assistance toward the return passage was given. While many did return to India, the majority remained to settle in the West Indies, either undertaking further periods of indenture or working as free laborers, taking up land, or moving into other occupations. Substantial numbers of East Indians went to Jamaica, Guadeloupe, Martinique, and Surinam (which, after the ending of Indian indentures, continued importing Asiatic labor from Java), and smaller numbers to French Guiana and the British Windwards; but the overwhelming majority went to the less developed British territories of Trinidad and British Guiana, where they soon predominated among the labor force in a sugar industry which still had the ability to expand, and where they increased in number to constitute a very substantial element of the population in the present century. Puerto Rico was also undergoing substantial expansion of the sugar industry in the mid-nineteenth century, and there too labor was required. Although the slaves were not freed until 1873, the slave trade had been abolished before there was a very significant Negro population. Some labor was obtained by the migration of planters and their slaves from the Virgin Islands, and this was supplemented by government regulations which forced the peasant population of the island to work in the sugar industry.

Indentured labor in British Guiana and Trinidad and forced labor in Puerto Rico meant the continuance of something akin to the slave plantation society. Though the condition of the indentured laborer, unlike that of the slave, was temporary, he was subject to many restrictions on his personal liberty and had little opportunity to participate in the wider society outside the plantation, on which he had to reside, and which he could not leave without permission. He was liable to imprisonment for breach of a variety of minor regulations, and planters appear to have found the threat of pressing charges a useful lever to secure re-indenture. The interest taken by the British and Indian governments in the fate of the indentured workers and the provision of officials with responsibilities for the welfare of Indian immigrants prevented the system from degenerating into a virtual continuation of slavery, without, however keeping it free of abuse. The forced laborers of Puerto Rico were less fortunate, and their lot appears to have been little different from that of the Negro slaves alongside whom they worked. The indenture system introduced the Asiatic element into West Indian society in rather inauspicious circumstances. There was some resentment of the Indian, as his presence tended to force down the price of wage labor, but more important was the contempt of the Negro for the "coolie," who was prepared to undertake the field labor which the Negro associated with slavery; and the Indian was also liable to be despised for his religion by Negroes recently converted to evangelical Christianity. Racial stereotypes thus developed which have persisted in large measure to the present and have retarded social integration, especially in Trinidad and the Guianas.

If indenture enabled plantation society to persist in modified form in some territories, the plantation generally ceased, after emancipation, to be the dominating social instituion of the West Indies (though it did, of course, continue in many territories as a system of agriculture). In the first place, as already indicated, many former slaves quickly became emancipated geographically or occupationally as well as legally. In Jamaica especially, but also in other territories, freedmen left the estates for the hills or other areas remote from the surviving sugar plantations, acquired plots of land, and set up as independent agricultural producers, farming for subsistence or for local, or even export, markets, often eventually employing some wage labor, and thus enabling others to free themselves from the estates. Contact between such communities and the plantations was often minimal. Others moved to coast or market towns and maintained an often precarious existence in the service occupations to which the more variegated economic pattern that emerged gave rise. Many became semi-independent and divided their time between small holdings and sporadic wage work for the planters, their relationship with whom thus became purely economic. Even those who found it most difficult to break away, and had to continue to live on or near estates, usually did their best to evade social control by asserting their liberty to sell their labor to the employer of their choice.

Perhaps the most significant social change was the growing dissociation of women and children from the plantations. Women had often formed a sizable element in field gangs, but relatively few appear to have continued in this sort of work for long after emancipation. They devoted themselves rather to homemaking and tending their family small-holdings. The children's gang, too, which did light work on the plantations but was often regarded more as a liability than as an asset, did not survive emancipation. While children would generally work on family plots, many parents preferred to send them to school to "better themselves" rather than to the estates to undertake "slave work."

These changes gave the family the opportunity to emerge as the basic social unit. Under slavery anything approaching normal family life had often been impossible, though in the later years, and especially after the abolition of the slave trade, when replacements to the labor force had to be bred instead of imported, some development of the family had taken place, but still within a very limiting context. The family structure which did emerge from slavery proved to be highly flexible, with the nuclear family living in Christian marriage perhaps the ideal but seldom the norm. For this development various explanations have been offered, each of which tends to concentrate on a different aspect of the institution: the reluctance to contract formal marriage bonds has been attributed to a reaction against the binding force of the relation between slave and master; the impermanence of many unions to the habit of transient relations originally promoted by the realities of slave existence; the matriarchal focus to elements in the African heritage; and the matrilocal tendency to the economic inability of many, perhaps most, West Indian husbands in the century after emancipation consistently to sustain the role of resident breadwinner. Whether the post-emancipation West Indian family was an African retention, a conscious deviation from a European ideal, or a pragmatic response to West Indian conditions, it certainly gave rise to a much higher level of fertility than that which had prevailed under the inhibiting restraints of slavery. High death rates and low birth rates had been characteristic of West Indian slave society and had necessitated regular importations of slaves. While death rates may have fallen somewhat with the advent of freedom, the really significant change was the rising birth rate, which soon exceeded the death rate. The West Indian Negro population then began to expand by natural increase.

By the late nineteenth century rising populations were combining with economic depression to produce a migratory movement from the more crowded islands, especially Jamaica and Barbados, to places offering greater employment opportunities. Of these the most important was Panama. As early as the 1850s some thousands of West Indians had gone there on railroad construction work, and again in the 1880s much of the labor force for the abortive French attempt to dig an interoceanic canal came from the West Indies. Much the greatest, however, was the migration stimulated by the American canal construction between 1904 and 1914, in which over 20,000 West Indians were involved. Another significant movement was to Central America, where railroad construction and the development of the banana industry in Costa Rica and Honduras were going on from the last years of the nineteenth century. The rapid development of the Cuban sugar industry by United States capital after the end of Spanish rule also called for an immigrant labor force, especially in the second decade of the twentieth century. Throughout these years there was also considerable, if less systematic, migration to the more advanced and diversified economy of the United States.

Essentially this migration was of a purely temporary, work-seeking nature. Relatively few migrants intended to break their ties with their islands and settle permanently, though in practice a substantial minority did. Most worked for a few years, sending part of their earnings home to help support their families, and many returned perhaps after several spells in different places abroad, with savings adequate to establish themselves on a small farm or in a small business. The availability of such opportunities abroad provided a valuable safety valve against demographic pressure, until, in the 1920s, new immigration laws and changing economic circumstances in the United States and elsewhere closed up virtually every migratory outlet for the West Indies. Not only could new would-be emigrants find nowhere to go to, but many abroad were forced to return. The late nineteenth and early twentieth centuries thus saw immigration of East Indians to some parts of the area, and emigration of Negroes from other parts of it, but by about 1930 migration in either direction on any scale had ceased. From about 1920 death rates had started a steady decline, and the area had to face the world depression of the 1930s with a serious and growing overpopulation problem.

Emancipation naturally had its most far-reaching social effects on the slaves, and the consequent readjustments on the part of the free population were minimal. Although legal distinctions based on color generally disappeared around the same time as the ending of slavery, social distinctions continued to be largely so based, and possibly increased in rigidity. The depressed state of the sugar industry, on which the white population was largely dependent, led in many places to a decline in its size and wealth relative to the rest of the community, which in turn tended to produce an increased preoccupation with the status conferred by whiteness. The Afro-Europeans, who had been "free persons of color," and after emancipation were often referred to as "brown," were probably even more highly color-conscious. Those who were rising economically found their color a bar to the enjoyment of the full social fruits of their success and those who were not found their position threatened by successful Negroes. Both reacted by emphasizing their cultural identity with the whites and their separateness from the blacks, and sought the preservation and enhancement of their status by marrying persons of lighter skin to "improve the color" of the family. Thus social mobility was very difficult for the emancipated Negro. Generations of "marrying white" were required to overcome color disqualifications, and cultural acceptability was scarcely more easily acquired.

The persistence of colonial status ensured the continuance of metropolitan culture values as the standard for colonial society, but few facilities were developed for transmitting this culture to the mass of the population. In the early years of emancipation in the British territories, some optimistic attempts were made in this direction. The British government, for example, felt it important that the sugar industry should survive and flourish, lest, without the plantation as a focus of white civilization, the islands should "relapse into barbarism." In view of the planters' past record, these were pious hopes indeed, and the steps the Colonial Office was prepared to take were not enough, either to ensure the health of the industry or to prevent the freedmen from withdrawing from the plantations. More constructive was the metropolitan government's grant of funds for Negro education for a ten year period. This assisted the churches, already actively engaged in the task of bringing the Gospel to the ex-slaves, to set up schools through which, it was hoped, Christian civilization could be established, to be perpetuated through the training of native teachers and preachers. But when the British government's grant expired, the local governments which were left to take over the financing of education saw little utility in general education for the Negro masses. Ambitious educational plans had to be dropped in favor of "industrial" education for potential agricultural laborers. For the Negro population the education system offered little chance of access to the cultural world of the white and colored classes for whose benefit secondary schools teaching literary subjects for English public examinations, and often staffed with English teachers, were developed.

Even religion did not wholly succeed in providing common cultural ground. Although Christianity was, on the whole, enthusiastically accepted by the masses, the European missionary churches, especially in Jamaica, soon lost control of many of their members to native evangelical sects, which sprang up under half-educated Negro preachers. In many territories the freed Negroes evolved a Creole culture pattern of their own, which owed at least as much to the demands of the circumstances in which they found themselves as to African or European traditions or influence.

At the same time the "brown" and white upper classes followed metropolitan standards as slavishly as local circumstances would allow. This class and culture cleavage naturally produced mutual antagonisms, if seldom open conflict, and was no doubt a factor in such incidents as the Morant Bay "rising" in Jamaica in 1865 and the much more widespread and serious disorders of the 1930s, among the many consequences of which were the first really serious efforts to bridge the gulf which separated the West Indian classes and masses.

THE FREE ECONOMY

The ending of slavery, though primarily of social significance, also involved changes in the economy of most of the West Indian territories. In many islands there were substantial alterations in land utilization. Land unsuitable for estate cultivation was brought into use for the raising of minor export or food crops by freedmen who left the plantations. Other areas which could no longer grow sugar profitably were abandoned by the industry and were given over to other commodities (usually under new proprietors), split up among small farmers, or invaded by squatters. Although most land remained in the hands of large planters, they ceased to have a virtual monopoly of land ownership, and a substantial proportion of the population became proprietors of small parcels. Moreover, while sugar remained much the most important crop in most places, the use of different soils, terrains, and forms of land tenure led to more varied agricultural production.

As with land, so with labor. The breaking of the ties that bound the slave to the plantation enabled a variety of new occupations and labor relationships to emerge. But within the sugar industry, too, the change was marked. Slave labor had been proving progressively more expensive. Prices of imported slaves rose throughout the eighteenth century, and after the cessation of the slave trade planters had been faced with the even greater cost of raising slaves on their estates. The need to maintain a force to be on hand for the heavy demands of crop time, had encourged uneconomic labor practices during the remainder of the year. Thus, emancipation was far from being an unmitigated disaster for the sugar industry. In territories where there was little alternative to sugar estate work, emancipation could be a positive saving. In Antigua the planters calculated that by hiring labor only as and when they required it, they could produce more cheaply, and so they decided to dispense with the apprenticeship period and freed their slaves immediately. Where labor was scarcer or more expensive, emancipation provided a stimulus to the introduction of labor-saving devices, such as the plough, and to the maximizing of agricultural and industrial productivity, so that yields could be maintained with a smaller labor force. Labor, however, remained a considerable problem, as harvesting continued to necessitate a seasonal demand for large numbers of unskilled workers. Competitive market conditions restricted the planters' ability to attract workers by high wages, and they continued to try to ensure their labor supply by modifications of the traditional means of retention in the slack season and compulsion in crop time, through such devices as long-term indentures for immigrant laborers and tenancies conditional on estate work.

An even more compelling stimulus to economic change, however, was the ending of protection in metropolitan markets from, in the case of Britain, foreign competitors, and, in that of France, home-grown beet sugar. After 1850 the West Indian sugar industry was fighting for survival in a world market which it could no longer influence, dominated as it was by new large-scale producers such as

Brazil and Cuba. Although world demand was rising, so was supply, and the West Indies, with its traditional high-cost, low-grade product, was not geared for a market demanding cheap sugar of high quality. Greater efficiency, particularly by the adoption of new manufacturing techniques, was urgently called for. In British Guiana, Trinidad, and Puerto Rico, where the industry was relatively new and still expanding, capital was more readily obtained for the installation of new machinery. Even in Barbados the advantages of an ample labor supply and a vigorous resident planting class prepared to experiment and innovate outweighed the limitations of a small long-worked island. But in Jamaica, in the French territories, and in most of the remaining British islands, the necessary adjustment was too great for a large part of the industry to make, and only those few that were able and willing to undertake drastic modernization survived.

In the second half of the nineteenth century the West Indian sugar industry undoubtedly improved its efficiency considerably. There was substantial reorganization. Marginal estates, or parts of estates, were abandoned: properties were amalgamated to produce plantations of more economic size; ownership became concentrated in the hands of fewer individuals or companies. In the British West Indies, for example, the number of separately operated estates declined from some 2,200 at the time of emancipation to under 800 in 1900. Agricultural improvements, such as selective breeding of cane plants and greater use of fertilizers, increased yields of cane, but the really important advances were in manufacturing. Mills of more complex design, driven by steam or water in place of cattle or wind, were able to extract a much greater proportion of the cane juice, and the quantity and quality of sugar produced from it were much increased by the substitution of the vacuum pan and centrifugal drier for the more primitive equipment formerly used in the subsequent stages of manufacture. Because some estates were too small to take full advantage of some types of machinery, especially the larger mills, the method of manufacture by central factories was started in some areas and became virtually universal in the twentieth century. Such a factory served a number of estates, eliminating the wasteful duplication of expensive machinery and processing, and in some cases completely divorcing the management of growing from that of manufacture. The first centrals were constructed in the French islands around 1860, and the idea spread to Trinidad and St. Lucia, and, somewhat later, to Antigua and St.

Kitts. In British Guiana central factories were scarcely necessary. There the problem of sea defenses and land drainage along the coastal strip made small-scale sugar farming impracticable, and the estates were, for the most part, already large enough to justify a large modern factory for each. In Barbados, however, the tradition of the resident planter on his independent family estate, which had resisted the process of consolidation and amalgamation of properties which took place elsewhere, also delayed the introduction of a central factory system.

These various developments would probably have enabled the reorganized West Indian sugar industry to meet fair competition in a free world market. The competition, however, did not remain fair, nor the market free. The late nineteenth century saw the dramatic development of the European beet sugar industry, especially in France, Germany, and Austria. The various governments, interested in national economic self-sufficiency, were prepared to encourage the expansion of beet production by paying producers a bounty on all sugar exported. The free British market was thus inundated with beet sugar priced below production cost, and the West Indians were undercut in their traditional markets. The British colonies had to turn for a market to the United States, which, unlike their own mother country, was protecting cane producers by means of a countervailing duty. This relieved the situation somewhat until the end of the century, when the United States acquired large sugar producing territories in the Pacific, as well as Puerto Rico, and proceeded to make preferential arrangements for these in the American market. While this led to great expansion of the Puerto Rican industry, it also involved effective exclusion for the British territories, and the abandonment of the bounty system by a European agreement of 1902 brought little relief, for by then the beet industries were so well established that they could hold their own in the British market without bounty aid. In the years immediately before World War I only a marketing arrangement with Canada saved the industry in the British islands. The cutback in beet production during World War I led to a temporary revival of West Indian prosperity, but this was followed by a disastrous slump in 1920 and by further fluctuations culminating in the depression conditions of the 1930s.

While sugar continued to be the most important West Indian crop, both the passing of the slave system and the difficulties encountered by West Indian sugar in world markets prompted some agricultural diversification. Even where sugar remained the dominant industry there was probably more local production of food crops and somewhat less reliance on imports than there had been under slavery; and where sugar declined, as in Jamaica and the Windward Islands, small farmers much more generally raised crops for their own subsistence and for local markets. But consumer preference, even among ex-slaves, for many kinds of imported foodstuffs remained high, and agriculture retained a marked export orientation. Diversification was thus not confined to supplying local consumption, but involved the development of new export crops, by both large and small farmers, even in such leading sugar colonies as British Guiana and Trinidad. In the former, rice cultivation was rapidly expanded in the early twentieth century, first to meet the home market demands for a food previously imported, and later to be exported in substantial quantities. In the latter, and in some other territories, cocoa assumed great importance as a secondary export crop, as did coffee in a number of islands. In some places sugar virtually ceased to be exported or was relegated to a subordinate place in the export economy, as for example in Grenada, where spices became the principal product.

Much the most important development of this sort was the cultivation of bananas in Jamaica. The fruit had long been known in the West Indies as a food, but its highly perishable nature had never been conducive to the development of an export trade. In the 1860s, however, vessels bound for various ports in the United States speculated in the purchase of a number of cargoes from small farmers. A ready sale was found for the bananas in the American market, and most of the shippers concerned returned for more. Small farmers, especially along the north coast of Jamaica, began to expand their cultivation, and by about 1880 several entrepreneurs were becoming regularly engaged in the trade. These were usually shippers who, besides their basic problem of conveying the fruit to its destination in good condition, had to enter into arrangements with producers in Jamaica to secure supplies, and with distributors in the United States to dispose of their cargoes. By the end of the century the banana business had expanded phenomenally and involved not only small farmers but also large planters. Most of the old sugar planters looked askance at banana production, which was associated with Negro peasant farming, but many abandoned sugar estates were brought into banana cultivation, often under new owners from the mercantile classes. The most successful of the entrepreneurs went into all phases of the business, owning plantations on which the cutting was carefully timed to meet the schedules of their steamships which had taken over transportation from the earlier sailing vessels, and which delivered to distributors in the United States who were under the same management. With the formation of the United Fruit Company in 1899 a virtual monopoly of the United States market was established, and the same firm controlled much of the banana growing in, and shipping from, the Caribbean area. Other Jamaican growers sought, with government help, to circumvent this monopoly by developing the British market, which had just become accessible with the introduction of refrigerated ships which could land the cargo at a much more distant port in satisfactory condition. But the subsidized shipping line failed within a few years and was taken over by United Fruit, which thus controlled all Jamaican banana exports until 1929, when a growers' association was able to make independent shipping arrangements. Before the end of the nineteenth century bananas had become a much more important export item to Jamaica than sugar and continued to play a great part in the economy, providing not only employment on plantations, but cash income to a large number of small farmers.

Diversification was not confined to agriculture. In the early twentieth century mineral resources began to receive some attention. The growing importance of petroleum led to exploration in Trinidad as a possible source within the British Empire. Investigations proved successful, and exploitation started just before World War I, and expanded thereafter to account for more than half the island's exports in the 1930s. The reduced dependence on tropical agriculture gave the economy of Trinidad a greater buoyancy than most other territories enjoyed in this period. Even more significant was the effect of petroluem developments on the Netherlands Antilles. Commercially important in the days of intense national rivalries, these barren islands lacking in agricultural resources had languished in the nineteenth century. But the beginning of the exploitation of the immense oil fields in the Lake Maracaibo area of Venezuela gave them a new lease on life. Both political and geographical considerations deterred the great international oil companies from setting up refineries on the mainland. Safer havens were found in these offshore islands, and in the 1920s

Royal Dutch Shell in Curaçao and Standard Oil in Aruba built two of the largest refineries in the world.

Bauxite extraction in the Guianas began in the same period, with the developing demand for aluminum. In British Guiana production started in 1917, and in Surinam a few years later, and by the 1930s these two territories were among the world's largest producers, supplying much of the needs of the North American aluminum industry. Although their operations employed little labor, the bauxite companies contributed substantially to the colonial treasuries.

While these various new products did something to offset the difficulties experienced by sugar, making some of the territories less dependent on the world market for any single commodity, the hundred years culminating in the depression of the 1930s were characterized by stagnation rather than growth. Population, especially in the later years of the period, tended to increase faster than national income, and living standards probably fell, especially after the closing of emigration outlets. The generally depressed state of the West Indian economy is certainly to be explained to some extent by changing world conditions; partly, too, by the attitudes toward production of both freedmen and planters in the post-emancipation era; but perhaps most of all by the economic views of the metropolitan governments, and in particular that of Britain, the country responsible for most of the area. The nineteenth-century British policy of *laissez faire*, which persisted, by and large, until 1932, was no doubt well adapted to the expanding economy of the mother country, but it had little applicability to a depressed and overpopulated colonial area. The free working of the profit motive meant little investment or trade for the Caribbean. So far did the British government carry its inhibition against interference in the economy that, in the case of beet sugar, it would not even retaliate against governments which acted in direct contravention of free trade principles. In such an atmosphere, direct assistance to rehabilitate stagnant economies could not be expected. Acute distress might be relieved as an act of charity, limited subsidies might be given for short periods, loans might be advanced for actuarially sound projects, but governmental encouragement could often amount to no more than exhortation. Only when the experience of the 1930s brought the problems of depression forcibly before the metropolitan countries was any sort of sympathetic understanding of West Indian economics possible. Until then the deviation of metropolitan ideas and Caribbean realities continued and assumed more significance as, in most places, not only did conservative planters remain the dominant influence in colonial politics, but metropolitan political control and colonial political dependence tended to increase.

The Politics of Dependence

The social and economic changes which flowed from emancipation inevitably had political consequences. In the heyday of slavery in the eighteenth century, the white planting classes were economically in a position of unchallenged dominance. This they carried over to the social sphere by legally entrenching a caste system based upon race, which involved limitations on the civil rights of free persons of color. In these circumstances it was easy for them to hold a monopoly of political representation and influence over the local organs of government, which enjoyed a fair degree of liberty in managing local affairs. By the mid-nineteenth century, however, this situation had changed substantially. In many territories the marketing and labor difficulties encountered by the sugar industry made the planters economically weaker. Even where they were not so in any absolute sense, they generally held a relatively less dominating position in the more varied economies, in which independent Negro farmers and middle-class colored merchants had carved out places for themselves. The removal of legal distinctions based on color had, even before emancipation, opened the way for the colored middle classes not only to acquire considerable wealth, but also to rise in the social scale and play a part in political life by acquiring the qualifications necessary to intrude into the formerly exclusively white island oligarchies. The abolition of color discrimination in law meant that, on obtaining their freedom, slaves entered on an inheritance of full citizenship. In the nineteenth century, however, the rights of the citizen did not necessarily include that of direct political representation through personal voting powers, and in practice in most territories the freedmen were denied the vote through restrictive property or income qualifications for the suffrage. Both the white and colored segments of the oligarchy were likely to be able to agree on keeping the mass of the ex-slaves out of politics. But while, in the short run, the maintenance of an oligarchic political system presented no great difficulty, in the long run the liberated masses could be expected to make the influence of their numbers felt. The fear of slave rebellion, which had colored all eighteenth-century planter thought and action, was replaced after emancipation by the scarcely less horrifying specter of black democracy.

The political predominance of the colonial upper classes was threatened not only by the latent challenge of the ex-slaves but also by changing metropolitan attitudes. In the eighteenth century the colonies had enjoyed a substantial measure of control over local affairs, within the framework of imperial economic systems. But the revolutions in the mainland colonies of North America and in Saint-Domingue produced a reaction in Europe toward closer metropolitan control, which was intensified by colonial resistance to humanitarian antislavery policies. The strength of colonial opposition to amelioration and emancipation suggested that colonial autonomy would lead to oppression of the submerged majorities by the oligarchies, and that, to prevent this, metropolitan authority should be increased rather than diminished.

In the case of the French territories this was eventually brought about by their complete integration into metropolitan France. The fluctuations of French domestic politics in the mid-nineteenth century produced some inconsistencies in colonial policy, but in general, although there were times when moves were made toward colonial autonomy and *laissez faire*, the trend was toward closer control and a rather doctrinaire assimilationism. When this coincided with radical domestic politics, it involved the extension of the franchise to all colonial as well as metropolitan Frenchmen, even though the former were very largely recently liberated Negro slaves. This did not, however, lead to black democracy in the French colonies, but rather to black participation in an overwhelmingly white metropolitan democracy. Assimilation, which became settled policy in the 1870s, meant centralized metropolitan control over all important issues and left little more than municipal matters in local hands. With the island governments concerned rather with administration than policy, the mass of the population was, for many years, apathetic about the exercise of its voting rights. The colored group tended to monopolize political life and compete for minor offices, while the white element (whose significance was greatly reduced by the wiping out of their largest community at St. Pierre in Martinique in the 1902 volcanic eruption of Mont Pelée—perhaps the most dramatic natural disaster in Caribbean history) largely withdrew from politics, secure in the knowledge that even if the metropolitan government did not exactly protect their interests, it was not likely to countenance their oppression by the majority.

In the British territories a similar outcome was achieved by rather different means. Development there was influenced by the less radical constitutional views, current in Britain at the time, that the franchise should be restricted to persons of property or education—the "respectable" part of the nation. Thus there was little enthusiasm in British circles for preventing the possibility of oligarchical excesses by extending the franchise to the uneducated masses. Rather, it was held that government should be carried on impartially by the Colonial Office in London in the interests of the whole colonial population, until education and property were sufficiently diffused to ensure that a representative system would be reasonably responsible and democratic. This implied, in the case of a newer colony like Trinidad where no elected body had been set up, that demands from the English community for representative institutions should be turned down. The problem was more difficult with the older colonies. After the failure of an attempt by the Colonial Office in 1839 to get the British Parliament to override the rights of the old-established colonial representative assemblies by suspending the Jamaican constitution, the officials could only scrutinize colonial laws very carefully and disallow any felt to be unduly oppressive. In most of these islands, however, pressure on the oligarchy, and particularly on the white element in it, tended to increase with the decline of the sugar industry and the failure to make adjustments to the new social situation. Control was beginning to pass to colored mercantile groups, some elements of which were beginning to make a bid for mass support from the unenfranchised multitude. In these circumstances, the riots at Morant Bay in Jamaica in 1865 had consequences out of all proportion to their significance. What was intrinsically a minor local affair was represented by the governor as an attempt at a concerted rising of the blacks from end to end of the island, aided and abetted by colored demagogues. In the panic thus engendered, strong government was called for, and the governor was able to induce the Jamaican legislature to abolish itself and hand over all its powers to the British government. Nor were the effects confined to Jamaica. The same panic and reaction spread to the eastern Caribbean colonies which, within a few years, also surrendered their old assemblies. Only the Barbados assembly survived. On that island the white population was proportionately much larger; the sugar industry continued to dominate, and even to prosper modestly; and, by retaining their economic position, the white planters were able to preserve their social and political predominance as well. With this exception, and those of British Guiana, which until 1928 had a unique constitution inherited from the Dutch administration, and the Bahamas, with a different social and economic structure, all the British colonies had passed under direct Colonial Office control by the 1870s.

This control was exercised through the Crown Colony type of constitution, whereby the colonial lawmaking body was a legislative council nominated by the governor and consisting largely of colonial service officials. Control was scarcely less complete when, at various times in the different colonies, the composition of the councils was modified to admit a number of elected members, as these could normally be outvoted by the governor's nominees, and were in any case elected from a franchise narrowly restricted by property or income qualifications. The adoption of the Crown Colony form of government by the action of the colonial assemblies themselves meant essentially that the white oligarchies sacrificed the traditions of colonial self-government and aspirations toward a greater colonial autonomy which seemed likely to be dominated by others than themselves, in favor of a dependence on a metropolitan government which they hoped to be able to influence. This hope was not disappointed. Although the Colonial Office was enthusiastic in embracing the opportunity of trying to do more for the colonial masses than the local assemblies had done, the Crown Colony system was ill-adapted to bring about any fundamental social or economic change, being heavily biased in favor of the maintenance of the status quo. It generally failed to utilize the intimate knowledge and active concern of all but the most conformist and conservative of colonials. Decision-making was largely in the hands of the Colonial Office, which had to rely for guidance on colonial service personnel who were moved frequently from place to place within the Empire and seldom spent long enough anywhere to develop detailed knowledge of a particular colony. The colonial civil servant's natural social contacts were with the leading white citizens, whose image of the colony and its people he was most liable to adopt. He was unlikely, if he valued his career, to risk stirring up a hornet's nest. Where an exceptional governor did so, his unorthodox influence could still be counteracted by direct lobbying of the Colonial Office by those in England with West Indian business interests. With London more and more the source of political rewards and favors, the interests of the élite became centered on the metropolis rather than on the colony; and these political developments worked to accentuate the cultural gap between the élite and the masses.

Alienation between governors and governed reached its most acute form in Puerto Rico. Under Spanish rule the colonial élite had been less fundamentally divorced from the masses, which contained a smaller element of slave origin than most other islands. Indeed, the colony's leaders had themselves taken the initiative in emancipation. A colonial nationalist movement developed in the nineteenth century which finally won a substantial measure of local autonomy from Spain in 1897. But within a year the United States had taken over the colony, which it proceeded to administer with little consistent regard for other than strategic considerations (the island was the responsibility of the War Department until 1933) and the Washington influence of the American business interests that soon acquired a large share of the island's sugar industry, which they rapidly expanded. While there was little nostalgia for Spanish rule, Puerto Rican hopes of immediate assimilation into the democratic structure of American government were swiftly dashed by the decision to make the island an "unincorporated" territory which could not look forward to early statehood and whose inhabitants were not American citizens. The privilege of citizenship was accorded in 1917 along with other constitutional advances, including a bicameral elected legislature, but Puerto Rico remained very much a dependency, in practice subject in all important issues to the will of the United States Congress, in which it was not represented, and with its Governor and some other officials nominated by the United States President. The American régime thus tended toward neither assimilation nor autonomy, although it could be manipulated to a great extent by the wealthy classes to maintain, as far as possible, their economic and social position. But the Spanish élite of Puerto Rico naturally found it much more difficult to identify with the United States as the focus of their aspirations and the source of their cultural values than did the British and French élites with their mother countries. While some became strong advocates of Americanization, even to the point of supporting the American policy of trying to make Puerto Rico English-speaking by decreeing the use of English as the medium of instruction in Puerto Rican schools, most had to content themselves with belonging to a subculture generally viewed as inferior by the Americans who came to rule and to exploit the island.

The American acquisition of Puerto Rico was one manifestation of increasing United States interest in the Caribbean area. The British dominance, achieved by 1815, had brought to an end nearly three centuries of European rivalry, and it was not until the middle of the century that the United States began to offer any real challenge. This arose, in the first place, over communications through Central America to the newly acquired Pacific territory of California. It seemed at the time urgently necessary to build an interoceanic canal, but when the United States began to take steps in this direction it was found that much of the Caribbean coast of the isthmus was under effective British domination. British interest in this area dated back to the seventeenth century and, after sporadic conflict with Spain for about a hundred years, a settlement had finally been reached in 1786, whereby British settlers were permitted to cut wood in a defined zone comprising part of the present territory of British Honduras (which remained under Spanish sovereignty) if they agreed to evacuate settlements in other parts of the area. During the Napoleonic Wars a Spanish attack on the British zone had been beaten off and the area of British settlement increased. Spanish sovereignty was never successfully reasserted before Spanish interest in the area practically ceased with the independence of Central America and Mexico in 1821. In 1836 Britain attempted to induce Spain to cede to her the sovereignty of the enlarged territory that was effectively under her jurisdiction, but no action was taken and, with claims coming from both Mexico and Guatemala, the international status of the area was indeterminate for some years.

In the 1840s British *de facto* authority was extended to the Bay Islands (commanding the Atlantic coast of Honduras) and the Mosquito Shore of Nicaragua, including the mouth of the San Juan river, the most probable Atlantic terminal for an interoceanic canal. The Americans at first assumed that British expansion in Central America had been undertaken with a view to monopolizing interoceanic transit, but later found that Britain was not disposed to try to uphold any such monopoly and was prepared for a partnership with America in a region she had previously dominated. In a treaty of 1850 the two countries agreed to cooperate over a canal, which would not be exclusively controlled, and to neutralize Central America by refraining from colonizing there. Although the canal rapidly receded as an important issue, serious and dangerous disagreements arose in the 1850s over the interpretation of the treaty, the United States holding that Britain was obliged to withdraw from her Central American territories, and Britain maintaining that the prohibition applied only to future colonization. By 1860, however, a compromise had been reached, whereby Britain abandoned the Bay Islands and the Mosquito Shore, and the United States acquiesced in her retention of a British Honduras much larger than the original area of the Spanish concession. Two years later Britain formally assumed sovereignty by declaring British Honduras a colony, an act which passed without protest from the United States.

Britain's other mainland territory, British Guiana, provoked another Anglo-American clash in the 1890s when the United States was persuaded to intervene in a dispute between Venezuela and Britain over the boundary between the republic and the colony. After an offer to mediate had been snubbed by Britain, the United States declared its intention of arbitrating itself, whether Britain agreed or not, and of taking any necessary steps to enforce its decision. When Britain, unwilling to risk war over such an issue, then proceeded to accept an arbitration procedure, another important step toward American hegemony in the Caribbean area had been taken.

By the end of the century, faced with a menacing situation in Europe and intensified imperial rivalry on other continents, Britain was prepared to pin her faith on Anglo-Saxon solidarity (a sentiment that was far from entirely reciprocated in America), in ceasing to compete and yielding supremacy in the Western Hemisphere to the United States. Thereafter events moved rapidly. Spain was defeated in the Spanish-American war of 1898, and the United States acquired Puerto Rico outright and a dominating influence over Spain's other Caribbean colony, Cuba, which gained a nominal independence. Britain gave up her treaty interest in an isthmian canal and conceded exclusive control to the United States. The beginning of work on the Panama canal, which followed in 1904, made the whole Caribbean area one of direct strategic concern to the United States. From then until the 1930s the United States sought to forestall any possible strategic threat from any European power by itself intervening militarily to preserve order and payment of international obligations in a number of the independent states of the area, and, in one case, by acquisition of territory. This was the Danish Virgin Islands, which, during World War I, appeared threatened by German designs and which passed under American sovereignty by purchase in 1917.

While the acquisition and retention of the United States Caribbean colonies is thus intelligible in strategic terms, the continued existence of colonies of European powers is less easily explained, especially after the end of the nineteenth century when they were, for the most part, of neither strategic value nor economic benefit and, indeed, in some cases required metropolitan financial support. There were, of course, some who profited from the connection both in the colonies and in the mother countries. The colonial link helped to sustain the social dominance of the white elements in the colonies, and it was they who usually had the greatest influence over their metropolitan governments. While there might be at times a rather generalized anti-imperial sentiment in a mother country, this could seldom be as effective as the vociferous activities of those with vested interest in the colonies.

But there were also broader factors at work. Metropolitan sentiment was more often pro-imperial, and there was a certain constructive sense of missionary purpose in nineteenth-century European colonialism, involving the urge to share the "blessings of civilization" with peoples overseas who were technically and culturally "backward." This perhaps reached its fullest expression in the French territories, with the idea of assimilation of dependencies into metropolitan France, and of so influencing and educating Negro West Indians that they would become no less French than Parisians. If the British and Dutch were not so ambitious and tended to concentrate less on culture than on law and order, they still saw it as the responsibility of the colonial powers to transmit the capacity for good government and civilized life to colonial peoples, so that they might eventually evolve to a stage where they could manage their own affairs and participate on an equal, or almost equal, basis in a wider British or Dutch community.

Such concepts, of course, applied to empires of which the West Indies were only a small part. It is noteworthy that the Scandinavian nations, with smaller imperial responsibilities, pulled out of the West Indies in this period. Sweden transferred St. Bartélemy to France in 1877, and as early as 1867 Denmark was prepared to sell the Virgin Islands to the United States. But where imperial responsibilities were vast, it was both practically much easier to administer a few small islands and psychologically more difficult to admit failure

*

and withdraw, even where the progress of the civilizing mission, hampered by financial stringency and static political systems, seemed slow and the territories were economic and strategic liabilities rather than assets. To a great extent the long senescence of European colonialism in the West Indies is to be explained by the habit of empire.

```
┌─────────────────────────────────┐
│                                 │
│              SIX                │
│                                 │
│                                 │
│   DEVELOPMENT AND AUTONOMY       │
│                                 │
│                                 │
└─────────────────────────────────┘
```

The 1930s mark an important turning point in the history of the West Indies. Thereafter, change in almost every aspect of West Indian life was rapid, in contrast to the static century which preceded. Population increased at a much faster rate, social services expanded tremendously, economies diversified and grew, real incomes rose, political participation became almost universal, and in most cases some form of self-government was achieved. All these changes were, however, manifestations of more fundamental changes in attitudes and climates of opinion both in the area itself and in the world at large. The depression of the 1930s revealed the limitations of free enterprise economics, and gave the lie to the nineteenth-century assumption that if wealth was looked after, welfare would take care of itself. On both sides of the Atlantic there was a much enhanced degree of acceptance for governmental intervention in the economy and the provision of social services. On the political side, the ideological implications of the allied cause in World War II, and some of its actual events, promoted a general tendency toward retreat from colonialism on the part of metropolitan powers, which was urged on by world opinion and acquired something of a momentum of its own. While the West Indies, in common with other colonial areas, was influenced by these trends, their local effects were decisively affected by the rise of broad, popularly based nationalist movements in the various West Indian territories.

THE RISE OF WEST INDIAN NATIONALISM

Modern West Indian nationalism was, and remains, a complex phenomenon, embracing within its ambit much more than the simple urge for freedom from metropolitan control. In the colonial context, any movement of popular protest against social and economic conditions was almost bound to take a political, and indeed nationalistic, form. Little change in the economy or the society could be expected in a political system geared to maintain the status quo. Only by obtaining political power could those interested in promoting reforms hope for much success. As local power was in the hands of metropolitan-oriented élites, and as authority ultimately lay with metropolitan governments, popular political movements necessarily involved an element of anticolonial nationalism.

The circumstances of the 1930s gave West Indians plenty to protest about. Almost everywhere in the area the impact of the world depression was very severe. Unemployment, already a problem in many territories, reached even more serious proportions, and real incomes fell to dangerously low levels. In Puerto Rico the local activities of the New Deal agencies set up to combat depression in the continental United States produced some immediate relief but little lasting effect, due largely to the obstruction of insular vested interests. By 1936 the United States administration had lost the interest it had briefly shown in Puerto Rican problems and was reverting to rather repressive authoritarianism, and there was a suggestion of immediate independence without economic aid. Between 1934 and 1938, most of the British territories experienced strikes, disorders, and riots, mainly started by workers in the sugar and other industries agitating for higher wages. Though basically economic in their demands and immediate origins, these disturbances were also symptomatic of widespread social and political frustrations throughout the region. West Indian consciousness of the inadequacy of the prevailing social standards was growing, due in part to increased contact with higher levels of living through overseas service in World War I and migration to the United States and elsewhere. The lack of adequate housing, water supplies, sanitation, education, and health services was made more evident by the increasing demographic pressure which resulted from falling death rates and returning immigrants. Hard times threatened the independence of the small peasant farmer, and made it easier for his innate individualism to be overcome and his latent resentment against the big landowner to be aroused by political leaders, who often combined genuine indignation at social injustice with the wish to obtain mass political support. The economic class antagonism both of the small man against the large and of the wage-earner against the employer developed strong nationalist overtones where the employer or landowner was, as so often, a metropolitan company.

Discontent with the existing state of affairs, especially for labor, was heightened during World War II. In much of the area American activity increased—for example, with the construction of air bases on the British islands under the "destroyers-for-bases" agreement of 1940. The high standards of living of American personnel, the high wages paid on base construction projects, the contrast between American labor-relations practices and the traditional paternalistic habits of island employers, and the scale of capital equipment and labor-saving devices used, all tended to bring home to the West Indies the potentialities for change.

In addition to concrete grievances over economic and social conditions, racial factors began in the second quarter of the twentieth century to exert a powerful influence on West Indian protest movements. The Negro "renaissance" of the 1920s in the United States, and in particular the ideas and activities in America of the Jamaican, Marcus Garvey, who returned to the West Indies in 1927, contributed significantly to the enhancement of the West Indian Negro's self-image. Garvey's United Negro Improvement Association was concerned with fostering a fierce pride of race, reasserting the Negro's African heritage, rejecting white values, and, at its most visionary, repatriating the Negro race to an independent African homeland. Also influential, if less directly than Garvey's movement which was aimed at the black masses of the world, was the literary and philosophical exploration of Negro identity, spreading from Haiti to the French West Indies and French West Africa, culminating in the complex of ideas that later came to be known as "*négritude*," in which the positive human vitality of the black race was extolled above the dehumanized, technically and materially obsessed condition of the white. Among some, these influences produced a violent, chauvinistic, antiwhite prejudice, but much more generally they contributed to an increased resentment against an unjust social system embodying *de facto* color discrimination. In a broader perspective, they formed part of the gradual process of psychological emancipation of the Negro from the stereotype of racial inferiority, deriving from slavery and persisting under continued European colonial domination.

That the popular discontents which thus came to a head in the 1930s were able to resolve themselves into effective mass organizations was perhaps indicative of the rising confidence of West Indian nationalism and the diminishing conviction of metropolitan colonialism. In the British territories, where the mass of the population was unenfranchised, organization in the first instance took the form of labor unionism. Several small trade unions, mainly of a specialized nature, had been in existence in the various British territories from early in the century, but in the late 1930s large general unions, embracing unskilled workers from different industries, began to emerge and to aim at large-scale coordinated action against the big metropolitan or international concerns that dominated many of the island economies. At the same time, middle-class professional people with political leanings were beginning to organize political parties with specifically nationalist aims. Such groups could give the organizational leadership and sometimes the financial assistance which the mass unions required, while the unions could give the politicians a mass basis of support. Trade unions and political parties thus developed in close association with each other, with the unions, able to act immediately on the industrial front, rather more important than the parties, which could not gain legislative representation under a restrictive franchise system.

In Puerto Rico, on the other hand, the mass of the population had had political rights for some time but had tended to sell their votes to the highest bidder rather than to exploit their powers in an organized fashion. There the effect of the events of the 1930s was to throw up a political party of a new type, which drew its strength from the charismatic impact of its pragmatic leader, Luis Muñoz Marín, on the rural masses rather than from successful jobbery and the support of vested interests. Muñoz's Popular Democratic Party (PDP) was pledged to bring about social and economic changes for the benefit of the voters, and, after gaining a precarious control of the Puerto Rican legislature in 1940, it was able to embark on its reformist program. This might not have got very far, had it not been for the appointment in 1941 of an American governor, Rexford Guy Tugwell, who thoroughly sympathized with Muñoz's aims and was prepared to cooperate with him in pursuing them. Not only this, but Tugwell was ideally qualified by his administrative experience and commitment to planning to forge a governmental machine that was fitted to meet the demands that social and economic development would place on it. The PDP received a massive vote of confidence in the 1944 elections, and when Tugwell left the scene in 1946 the retreat from colonialism that his policy foreshadowed was carried a stage further by the appointment of a Puerto Rican, and a supporter of Muñoz, as governor.

The changing attitude of the United States to Puerto Rico was perhaps more a consequence of Tugwell's activities than of any deliberate act of metropolitan policy. In the rather different circumstances of the British islands, metropolitan action was more significant. The British reacted to the disturbances of the 1930s by sending out a Royal Commission in 1938, whose revolutionary recommendations abandoned the idea of colonial financial self-sufficiency and proposed not only capital expenditure by Britain, aimed at developing the economies of the West Indian islands to a point where they could maintain their populations at a higher standard of living, but also grants to finance improved welfare services during the interim period in which development was taking place. The Commission further recommended constitutional changes to allow for greater local participation in government. Implementation of the economic and social aspects of the report was begun with the first Colonial Development and Welfare Act in 1940, and the rather modest constitutional recommendations were overtaken by the rapidly changing climate of opinion in World War II, which called for a much faster movement toward colonial self-government than had been envisaged in the late 1930s. The first-fruit of this change in the West Indies was the provision in 1944 of a new constitution for Jamaica embodying a legislature, the lower house of which was entirely elected from a franchise extended to include all adults.

The wartime occupation of the Netherlands meant that little change was practicable in the Dutch territories in the early 1940s. Nevertheless, the Dutch government-in-exile during the war made clear statements to the effect that postwar colonial policy would involve a considerably greater degree of devolution of metropolitan authority. More confused was the situation in the French territories, whose authorities took their lead from the neutral Vichy government and did not participate in the Free French movement. Whereas the Dutch territories were garrisoned by American troops, the French islands were so carefully watched by the Allies as to be virtually under a state of siege.

During World War II the metropolitan powers were naturally primarily concerned with the successful prosecution of hostilities (or, in the case of the French, preservation of neutrality). Although the colonial peoples in general showed an intense sentiment of loyalty toward the metropolitan powers and their cause, the war stimulated the nationalist movement in a number of ways. The subordination of colonial policy to metropolitan exigencies was highlighted; the suppression of some nationalist activities in the name of war emergency added the aura of persecution to the movement; and promises of changes at the end of the war gave some hope of success. By 1945 nationalism had become a force to be reckoned with in the Caribbean area.

DEVELOPMENT AND WELFARE

As a result of the events of the 1930s and early 1940s, both metropolitan countries and local political leaders throughout most of the area came to regard economic development as an imperative necessity. In the years following World War II some economic progress was made in almost every territory, but there was considerable variation in the degree of development achieved, due to great differences in resources and conditions as well as in ideas on the desirable lines of development and on the techniques for achieving it.

Undoubtedly the greatest strides were made by Puerto Rico. When Muñoz Marín founded the Popular Democratic Party and started campaigning, he deliberately played down the question of the constitutional status of the island and concentrated on economic and social questions, and he continued to do so after attaining power. Much of his concern was with the peasantry, from which his support derived, and it was not unnatural that one of the main planks of his platform was agrarian reform, specifically the implementation of a prohibition, originally enacted in 1900 but never enforced, against the ownership of more than 500 acres of land by any corporate body. Action under the terms of this law was popular not only with the agrarian population, who benefited from the break-up of large holdings, but also with nationalists generally, as the corporate landowners were most often continental American concerns. Even landed Puerto Ricans could indulge in nationalism, as the holdings of individuals, many of them very large, were not affected. While some land was redistributed in small parcels under this program, it was recognized that sugar production could only be organized profitably on a large scale, and most of the estates were turned into "proportional profit" farms which were run as units, but with the profits distributed among the workers in proportion to the amount of labor they supplied. The government also stimulated the introduction of new agricultural enterprises, notably dairy farming and the production and processing of pineapples for export.

But it was evident that, however socially desirable land reform might be, agricultural development was not likely to solve the economic problems of the overcrowded island. Industrial development had also been part of the PDP program and by 1942, when an industrial development corporation was set up, the main emphasis had moved in that direction. The times were reasonably propitious not only for the setting up of manufactures but also for doing so under public enterprise. Wartime shortages gave scope for import substitution industries, and the wartime boom in rum sales made revenues particularly buoyant, and so enabled the government to supply capital which was at that time forthcoming neither from the United States, whose economy was on a war footing, nor from wealthy Puerto Ricans, whose investments continued to be on the traditional lines of land and commerce. The development corporation thus went into the production of glass, paperboard, footwear, and clay products, besides taking over a cement factory which had been established under a relief program in the 1930s. Only the last of these prospered, and as some of the problems of industrialization became better understood, it came to be felt that progress under public enterprise was likely to be very slow.

After the end of World War II, the emphasis shifted toward the stimulation of private investment, with the government, which soon sold its factories to private concerns, playing a major role by developing public utilities, creating industrial estates, constructing factory buildings for lease or sale, providing facilities for training labor, and granting exemptions from taxation. In 1950 the whole development program, known as "Operation Bootstrap" or "Fomento," was placed under coordinated administration, and in the next decade some hundreds of industrial establishments were set up, involving investments of hundreds of millions of dollars, and employment for tens of thousands of workers. By 1956 the contribution of industry to the national product had outstripped that of agriculture and exports of manufactures exceeded those of sugar. Though manufacturing industry was much the most significant aspect of Puerto Rico's economic development, it was not the only one. Agricultural production was raised and diversified, and the island was made into the leading tourist resort of the Caribbean, catering not only, as formerly, to the very rich, but to the much wider sector of the American public that began to travel abroad on an enormous scale after World War II. By all these means, the island's economy between 1940 and 1960 was given a much broader base and the standard of living substantially increased.

To achieve this Puerto Rico exploited to the full the advantages of her relationship with the United States. Of these perhaps the most fundamental was the free entry of the island's products to the vast American market, protected by tariffs against virtually all other underdeveloped areas. Puerto Rico, with lower wage rates and surplus labor, was thus an attractive field for investment in labor-intensive industries, such as textile and garment manufacture, producing for sale in the continental United States. But with savings on wages offset by additional transport costs, free access was not in itself sufficient to stimulate large-scale investment. Fiscal incentives were also of crucial importance. Puerto Rico, being unrepresented in the United States Congress, was exempt from federal taxation, and in addition, had the power to regulate its own local finances, and was thus able to grant a ten-year exemption from local taxation to new investors. Furthermore, the Puerto Rican government was in a position to create conditions conducive to private investment by spending heavily itself on the infrastructure of the economy and on promotional activities. This was possible largely because of its eligibility for federal financial subventions (under a variety of schemes and agencies operating throughout the United States) on a scale many times that of the aid available to other territories from their metropolitan powers, as well as because of the remission to the Puerto Rican treasury of such items as the excise duty on Puerto Rican rum sold in the continental United States.

The great material progress which followed from the exploitation of these advantages was not achieved without substantial sacrifices of economic and political independence. Free access to the United States market for Puerto Rican products meant also free access to the island for continental products. Thus the manufacturing industries which developed were geared toward exports, rather than toward import substitution on the local market. Industrial development made Puerto Rico, if anything, even more closely dependent economically on the United States than before, with a substantial proportion of its industrial plant owned by subsidiaries of continental concerns and almost all of its external trade with the United States. As the nature of the economic development was such as to increase economic dependence, rather than promote a viable insular economy, its consequence was to make virtually impossible, in the foreseeable future, the complete political independence which had been the preferred constitutional objective of most of the new nationalistic political leadership, including Muñoz himself, until at least the middle 1940s. Even the alternative of complete integration in the form of statehood was made more difficult, as the consequent liability to federal taxation would have removed one of the important inducements to American concerns to invest in Puerto Rico rather than in some other part of the United States. Nevertheless, the economic development of Puerto Rico was an impressive achievement, the more so as it was engineered and administered almost exclusively by the Puerto Ricans themselves. Though Puerto Rico's unique advantages could not be paralleled elsewhere, and were the envy of the less fortunately placed territories, the island served as an example of what could be done, and some of the techniques developed there were copied in other parts of the region.

Significant economic developments also took place in the British territories, especially the larger islands, Jamaica and Trinidad. In the 1940s, before great political advances were made, policy-making and legislation were still largely in the hands of the metropolitan government, or expatriate officials. These, in general, tended to see the West Indies as an essentially agricultural area, and much effort was devoted to attempts to increase agricultural productivity, to secure markets for agricultural exports, and to reduce dependence on imported foodstuffs by raising more food locally. Some success was achieved in all these directions, but the rates of growth in the agricultural sectors of most territories were barely sufficient to maintain existing living standards in the face of rapid population growth, and showed no signs of being able to satisfy rising expectations.

Though industrialization on Puerto Rican lines was not without its advocates, the lack of easily accessible export markets in which preferential entry terms for manufactures could be expected operated to restrict consideration of industry largely to the processing of local food products for export, and import substitution for local markets. The opportunities in the latter direction, however, were considerably greater for the British territories, which could control their own external tariffs, than for Puerto Rico, to which American goods had free entry. Thus, although the local markets were uneconomically small, they could be protected, even against British manufactures, by high import duties. Many such industries, particularly in the food and clothing lines, were set up, often based on local raw materials, and for some years the more efficient of them had the prospect of expanding to a more economic size when the West Indies Federation permitted free movement of goods between its component parts. In spite of a general inclination among many politicians toward socialistic programs and a widespread fear of the dangers of foreign "exploitation," an influx of private capital appeared to be the most available means of development. Thus tax and other incentives were established to attract a certain amount of North American investment into manufactures for the United States market, despite its tariff barriers, and similar inducements lured some local capital into productive rather than distributive enterprises.

By the 1960s Jamaica and Trinidad had gradually built up industrial sectors that were contributing significant proportions of the national product but had not been transformed into manufacturing economies. Indeed, much of the improvement in the economic position of these two islands was due to relatively fortuitous developments—the discovery and large-scale extraction and processing of bauxite in Jamaica, which started in 1952 and within five years was providing half the island's exports, and the increase in oil refining capacity in Trinidad. Both of these developments assisted the balance of payments and government revenues, and, though not labor-intensive in operation, gave much employment during the construction period. Jamaica's economy was further diversified by a great expansion in the tourist industry in the 1950s. Considering the relatively low level of metropolitan financial aid available to the British West Indian governments for development (much of which was devoted to public utilities and to improving communications by land, sea, and air) and the restricted possibilities of their metropolitan market, the economic achievements of the larger British territories were remarkable. Moreover, although their economies remained highly dependent on international trade, their structure moved closer to that of a viable independent state than did that of Puerto Rico.

In the smaller British territories the problems were greater. Guyana, hampered by political troubles, achieved little expansion, though there was an increase in mineral extraction, and the development of some manufacturing. In the 1950s British Honduras, formerly dependent very largely on forest products, expanded its agriculture—especially sugar and citrus for export, as well as food crops for local consumption—to exceed its lumber production. Barbados, Antigua, and the Bahamas, fortunately endowed with good airport facilities as a result of World War II, developed a substantial tourist traffic. The remaining islands, despite considerable efforts, particularly in agriculture, could make little progress in overcoming the disadvantages of absolute smallness, rugged terrain, and poor communications, to which were added the uncertainties of their political future as a result of the failure of various schemes for federation.

The Dutch territories prospered during World War II, with heavy demands for the products of their oil refineries and bauxite mines. However, uncertainty about the future of the oil refining business, a result of Venezuelan insistence on a higher proportion of its oil being refined within its territory, led to concern about the future of the Netherlands Antilles, and diversification was sought through the development of tourism in Curaçao and of industries associated with the American-owned refinery in Aruba. Moreover, by the 1950s the metropolitan government, having been divested of other colonial responsibilities and having rehabilitated the Dutch economy, was in a position to extend financial assistance, particularly toward improving harbor and airport facilities. In Surinam the extraction and processing of forest products was developed and the most impressive project of the entire area was undertaken, with the assistance of American capital—the construction of a massive dam and hydroelectric plant to service an aluminum smelter to process local bauxite.

By contrast, little progress was noticeable in the French territories which were, in 1946, fully integrated as overseas departments of metropolitan France, which virtually monopolized their trade and provided guaranteed markets for their main crops of sugar and bananas. Foreign capital was not encouraged and economic activity remained virtually confined to agriculture. Despite often vociferous criticism from nationalist elements of the economic limitations of the French departmental system, integrationist sentiments continued to prevail, and concentration tended to be on relief rather than development.

In general, the economies of the area developed considerably between the 1930s and the 1960s, and substantial increases in gross national product were achieved. But per capita increases were less impressive, on account of the great rise in population which was one of the most marked characteristics of the period. Death rates, which had begun to fall slowly in many territories in the 1920s, dropped much more rapidly in the 1940s and 1950s, principally as a result of improved public health and sanitation which greatly reduced the incidence of malaria, typhoid, dysentery, and other diseases. In Puerto Rico, for example, the death rate dropped from 18.2 per thousand in 1940 to 6.6 per thousand in 1960, and in Jamaica, between

1944 and 1960, it fell from 14.9 to 8.8 per thousand. In most territories infant mortality rates fell even more sensationally than death rates. This factor affected not only the absolute size of the population, but its age distribution, and also had eventual effects on the birth rates. These showed less consistent trends, rising in some territories and falling in others, but always remaining high and ensuring that a very large element in the population—in some places more than half—was too young to contribute to the economy, while making demands on it for educational and other services.

In many territories the effects of these large natural increases on total population were somewhat mitigated by heavy external migration—from Puerto Rico to the United States, from the British islands to the United Kingdom, and, to a much lesser extent, from Martinique and Guadeloupe to France. In the fifteen-year period ending in 1960, migration was on such a scale that the annual average increase of population in many islands was restricted to under 2 per cent, as against a natural increase of over 3 per cent. More than a third of the natural increase of Jamaica over the period was offset by emigration, and emigration from Puerto Rico and Barbados exceeded natural increase in some of the peak years of the 1950s. In the early 1960s, however, changing conditions in the United States and restrictive legislation in the United Kingdom cut down this outlet to relatively insignificant proportions.

In a sense, emigraton may be seen as part of a more general movement of urbanization which was noteworthy within the area itself. Growth of population was very much faster in urban than in rural areas, although fertility rates tended to be higher in the country districts. The same factors producing urbanization—rural overpopulation and the expansion of opportunities in industry and services—were at work in drawing population from the smaller British islands to Trinidad, and also at times from the Lesser Antilles to the oil industry of Curaçao and Aruba. Population increase and redistribution intensified the most serious socio-economic problem of the area, unemployment. Even in Puerto Rico industrialization and emigration in the 1950s failed to reduce the percentage of the working force out of work, and in some other territories the situation probably worsened, not only in scale but also in character. Unemployment and underemployment had been common in most of the West Indies from soon after the ending of slavery but, as long as the population remained largely rural, some relief was always available by participation in marginal subsistence farming. Population pressure aggravated the rural problem, but the situation became even more serious for the landless and rootless urban unemployed, who were totally dependent on wage labor, charity, or crime for a living. In the appalling slums that developed around the larger centers of population, civilized living was virtually impossible. With ever larger cohorts of teenagers entering the labor market, the problem of development became not only the purely economic one of raising per capita income by creating more wealth, but also the more complicated one of creating more jobs in the process. Neither labor leaders nor politicians were able satisfactorily to resolve the dilemma between the long-term objective of modernizing the economy by the introduction of capital goods and the training of skilled labor, which could raise individual productivity and support high wage structures and acceptable standards of living, and the short-term need to contain or reduce unemployment, which called for traditional labor-intensive, low productivity methods, job-sharing, and chronic underemployment. Governments, in many territories major employers of labor, were under particular pressure, being asked by trade unions, often closely identified with the political parties in power, both to give a lead to private employers with high wages, modern methods, and good conditions, and to play a key part in relieving distress by make-work projects involving as many people as possible. The levels of economic development and of emigration between 1940 and 1960 simply did not suffice to fulfil the aspirations of a rapidly increasing population to full employment at a high standard of living.

The gap between expectation and realization would have been considerably greater had it not been for substantial metropolitan spending on social services. These were improved considerably beyond the levels that the West Indies could themselves provide out of the revenues their economies could support. In the American and French territories, the insular authorities had access to federal or central funds for such services as health, education, social security, and housing; and the British and Dutch governments financed capital expenditures, specialist officials, training schemes, and other projects from special funds set up by metropolitan treasuries. Possibly the most striking advances were made in the sphere of public health. Not only did improved control of disease have dramatic effects on death rates, but hospital accommodation was substantially increased, clinics established, and personnel trained, including, in Jamaica and Puerto Rico, doctors turned out by the new University medical schools. The construction of the University College of the West Indies, begun in Jamaica in 1948, was one of the major expenditures from Colonial Development and Welfare funds in the British territories, and the postwar expansion of the University of Puerto Rico was another significant educational development. Despite the formidable increase in the number of children of school age, educational provision in most territories succeeded in keeping pace, and the proportion of children attending secondary schools was generally increased. Housing, however, remained an unsolved social problem, despite government initiative in constructing low-cost homes for rent or sale and in providing generous metropolitan subsidization.

The emphasis on welfare was not without its critics. In particular, it was argued that health measures, by reducing mortality, simply increased the level of unemployment, and that priority should be given to economic development, which alone could generate the capacity to support improved welfare services. It was also noted that metropolitan capital expenditure on schools and hospitals often threw upon local authorities the responsibility of maintaining and staffing from their own resources establishments on a scale they could ill afford. Public demand, however, for social services, and especially for education, intensified, and with the growing political power of the masses, governments were often constrained to give priority to immediate concrete social improvements rather than to long-term development objectives.

Economic and social conditions undoubtedly improved considerably, but with Puerto Rico's per capita national income in the 1960s no more than half that of the poorest state of the American union, Jamaica's no more than a third of that of the United Kingdom, and many territories not half as well off as Jamaica, West Indian socio-economic aspirations remained far from satisfied.

Toward Self-government

The period saw greater progress toward the satisfaction of socio-political demands. These were focused in two particular directions: the democratization of the internal territorial governments, and the ending of the metropolitan relationships of colonial subordination. While there were considerable differences between territories, and conflicts of opinion within them, over the forms of government aimed at and the desirable timing of their realization, by the early 1960s solutions were in process of being arrived at, broadly in accordance with the expressed wishes of the inhabitants, so far as these could be ascertained.

The democratization of local political institutions entailed the control of local legislatures by democratic electorates, the control of local executives by elected legislatures, and the expansion of the powers of the local government over local affairs. In the British territories the first step was the extension of the franchise, previously restricted by property qualifications to a narrow group largely concerned with maintaining the colonial status quo. Adult suffrage was introduced in Jamaica in 1944, in Trinidad in 1946, in Barbados in 1950, and in the remaining territories within a few years. The result, almost inevitably, was to give representation to nationalist groups with mass popular backing, who successfully pressed for further constitutional reforms, which involved the progressive taking over by elected members of the legislative and executive functions previously discharged by Colonial Office officials, and culminated in a full cabinet system in which only the few matters reserved for metropolitan jurisdiction and the emergency powers of the governor differentiated the colonial constitution from an independent one. Much the same development took place in the Dutch territories immediately after World War II. In Puerto Rico, where there had long been a legislature elected on adult suffrage, the principal issue was the control of the executive. This was secured by an act of the United States Congress in 1947 which made the office of governor elective. A further act of 1950 retained in the hands of the Congress a wide range of federal matters, such as citizenship, tariffs, interstate commerce, and federal jurisdiction, but gave Puerto Rico the right to frame its own internal constitution and the management of its insular affairs.

These political gains, sometimes wrung with difficulty from a cautious metropolitan government in the face of resistance from colonial upper classes, enhanced the prestige of political parties and gave nationalist movements the political power with which to further their aims. In general, the parties proceeded with measures to promote economic development and improve social conditions, with considerably more energy, if occasionally less judgment, than the preceding colonial governments, providing a valuable means of channeling the creative energies of the West Indian peoples for national purposes. National considerations were, of course, often subordinated to questions of personal rivalry or party advantage, and there were cases of political corruption. In small societies with little experience of mass political activity, this was much less surprising than the fact that any other conduct was ever in evidence and that statesmanlike decisions were not infrequently made. While sanctions remained in the hands of colonial powers, most politicians were careful to work within the constitutional framework of the time, while agitating for changes within it.

Two significant exceptions were the British mainland territories. In British Guiana a new mass party, the People's Progressive Party (PPP), with a markedly left-wing orientation, obtained power at the first elections held under universal suffrage in 1953. Led by Dr. Cheddi Jagan, the PPP deliberately sought to clash with the governor and other official and nominated functionaries in order to expose the constitutional limitations under which the elected members had to operate. The PPP recognized none of the usual conventional limits on its discretion to legislate as it saw fit and to combine political responsibility with the fomenting of labor unrest. This uncooperative attitude together with the party's communist affiliations and ideological inclinations combined, in the highly charged cold-war atmosphere of the early 1950s, to provoke the suspension of the constitution after a few months, and it was not restored until 1961, when Jagan again won the elections. By this time, however, a large and predominantly Negro element had broken away from the PPP, which thereafter drew its support mainly from the East Indian population. The second PPP government was harassed by strikes and riots, and a prolonged period of disorder continued until the opposition obtained power after elections held in 1964 under a new system of proportional representation. In British Honduras, the mass People's United Party exploited the Guatemalan claim to the territory as an element in their anticolonial nationalist campaign against the British, and its leader, George Price, was expelled from the executive in 1957 for allegedly entering into negotiations with Guatemala over some form of association between the colony and the neighboring republic. Price later repudiated any idea of the territory becoming a Guatemalan dependency and came out in favor of independence within the Commonwealth. Retaining popular support, he was admitted to office again. In most of the other territories, however, orderly constitutional advance proceeded uninterrupted.

While general progress toward internal self-government on a democratic basis was satisfying one political aspiration, the even more important question of what form of status, affiliation, or relationship with metropolitan or other territories was to replace colonialism was causing controversy in almost every territory. Not until after 1960 was this issue permanently settled in any territory, and, in many, the final outcome remains a matter of doubt. Although the basic problems of smallness, poverty, and economic dependence were general, the metropolitan concepts of possible relationships, and the ideas of local political leaders, varied considerably, and a highly diverse pattern of quasi-colonial dependencies emerged.

In the French territories the integrationist tradition, under which for many years the Caribbean colonies had elected representatives to serve in the French legislature, was carried to its logical conclusion when, in 1946, the colonies were renamed overseas departments of France and their administrative structure assimilated to that of metropolitan France. The office of governor was abolished and the head of the administration in each territory became the prefect, who was responsible to the French Ministry of the Interior. At first officials of the various branches of government in the overseas departments communicated directly with the various ministries in Paris, but when problems arose from this procedure it was decided in the late 1950s to give the prefect more of a coordinating role. This made his position more like that of the old governor, and the impression of continuing colonialism was reinforced by the increase in the number of Frenchmen filling government posts in the islands, few West Indians having the necessary experience of the workings of the metropolitan administration. There was much vociferous local criticism of the departmental system, one of the leading figures being the poet Aimé Césaire, who represented Martinique in the French Chamber of Deputies and argued against integration both on nationalistic lines and on the grounds that racial differences made the assimilation of the West Indian Negro into European France an absurdity. Similar sentiments were voiced in other departments, and the local communist parties, which enjoyed a considerable measure of support, also opposed the departmental system. Most elections, however, appeared to indicate that this opposition did not represent majority opinion and that most of the population favored assimilation. Cases of the suppression of political parties and annulling of elections, however, took place, which threw doubt on the accuracy of any assessment of popular sentiment, as did the thorough commitment of the French administration to the assimilationist ideal. Opinion within the French territories clearly remained divided on whether the departmental system was a satisfactory solution to the political aspirations of French West Indians.

The Dutch government during World War II committed itself to working out a new constitutional relationship with the Netherlands overseas territories, and this was achieved in a lengthy process between 1946 and 1954. By 1950 the various internal constitutional alterations which had been made granted full internal self-government to Surinam and the Netherlands Antilles. In 1952 the Dutch constitution was amended to allow for the equal participation of the Netherlands and the two overseas territories in the framing of a fundamental charter laying down the relationship between them. The charter which eventually emerged in 1954 set up the tripartite Kingdom of the Netherlands, a constitutional monarchy in which the monarch, represented in the two overseas kingdsoms by an appointed governor, would act only on the laws of parliament and with the advice of ministers. The basic provisions of the charter laid down the procedure for dealing with affairs defined as Kingdom matters, as opposed to internal matters (including amendments to internal constitutions), which were the individual responsibility of each of the three constituent countries. The principal matters placed under the jurisdiction of the Kingdom as a whole were the conduct of foreign relations and defense and questions of citizenship. The Kingdom was also made responsible for the upholding of fundamental human rights and the maintenance of the rule of law. The determination of policy on Kingdom matters was entrusted to a Cabinet for the Kingdom, consisting of the cabinet of the Netherlands with the addition of a minister-plenipotentiary for each of the overseas countries. No direct representation of Surinam or the Netherlands Antilles was provided for in the Kingdom Parliament (which was in fact the Dutch Parliament), but it was laid down that it had to follow a special procedure when dealing with Kingdom matters, to enable the views of the overseas territories to be adequately expressed and taken into account. Such an arrangement was considered preferable by the overseas partners to weakening their own scarce resources in men of affairs by sending a number of representatives proportional to their population to deliberate in The Hague. In practice, cooperation among the three parts of the Kingdom extended to many more matters than the limited subjects reserved for Kingdom jurisdiction. With full control of their internal affairs, and a considerable influence over matters of concern to the Kingdom as a whole, Surinam and the Netherlands Antilles appeared to feel, for the time being at least, that the new arrangements represented a satisfactory compromise which enabled traditional links to be maintained without too severely limiting local independence of action.

In no territory did the problem of future status cause more heart-searching than in Puerto Rico. Better placed geographically than any of the other West Indian colonies from the point of view of integration with the metropolitan country, Puerto Rico was culturally perhaps the least assimilated, having a deep-rooted Spanish tradition, which half a century of American possession had modified but not eradicated. This factor placed formidable difficulties in the way of an integrationist solution on the French basis. On the other hand, the island's high degree of economic and financial dependence on the United States suggested that complete independence would raise substantial difficulties, and the relative insignificance of Puerto Rico, compared with the immense American union, gave little prospect that the degree of parity achieved by the Dutch territories in working out a middle way between colonialism and independence would receive much consideration by the United States. Although specific, mutually exclusive solutions to the status problem were not formally adopted by the major political parties until the late 1940s, traditionally there had been two attitudes toward the island's future, and these had formed an important basis of political division. One major political grouping aimed at loosening the United States connection, and was inclined toward complete independence, though not necessarily at any price, for it included elements that thought more in terms of local autonomy. The other, which was affiliated to the Republican party on the mainland, aimed at a closer relationship with the United States, with possible full incorporation in the Union as a state as its logical target.

The Popular Democratic Party, when it was set up by Muñoz Marín, was a new phenomenon, not only because of its mass popular support but also because of its concentration on economic and social questions rather than on the status issue. Nevertheless, there could be no doubt about the PDP's general orientation. Muñoz had been an independentist in the 1930s (though not prepared to accept the United States measure of 1936 which proposed to set the island loose without any special economic arrangements) and the PDP, though not clearly committed to early independence, manifestly favored, indeed almost assumed, independence as Puerto Rico's final goal. By 1946, however, it was becoming evident that economic development could only be accomplished swiftly by making full use of the peculiar advantages of the island's economic relationship with the United States, and Muñoz had apparently become convinced that the United States was not likely, in the foreseeable future, to grant independence on any basis that would be other than disastrous to his hopes for development. He argued that independence was pointless if it undermined the basis of the land's economy, and urged instead that the immediate goal should be a transitional arrangement which would give internal autonomy and maintain the existing economic connections until such time as the Puerto Rican economy was strong enough to support independence.

This was a great disappointment to many prominent PDP members, who had looked forward to early independence and, indeed, had formed a nonpartisan organization to agitate for stronger action in this direction. Their organization was denounced by Muñoz as a rival party and they were forced to withdraw from the PDP and form the Partido Independentista Puertorriqueño (PIP). Most supporters of independence, however, preferred to pin their faith on Muñoz and stay with the PDP, which continued to poll over 60 per cent of the votes in the next three quadrennial elections, and by 1960 the PIP's support, in 1952 nearly 20 per cent of the electorate, had dwindled to no more than 3 per cent. By this time independentism had become more an intellectual attitude than a practical political proposition, and the PDP had further modified its stand. In 1950 the United States Congress had given Puerto Rico the power to decide on its own internal constitution, and in the document that emerged in 1952 the island was designated a "Commonwealth" or "Estado Libre Asociado" (free associated state). Despite the considerable list of matters which remained within the province of the United States Congress, it was proclaimed that colonial status had ended.

In the following year, after notification that the United States administration would immediately recommend to Congress the granting of independence to Puerto Rico if at any time the Puerto Rican legislature resolved in favor of it, the United Nations agreed to regard Puerto Rico as no longer a non-self-governing dependency, and to regard its relationship with the United States as a mutually agreed free association. By 1954 it was being asserted by the Puerto Rican legislature that commonwealth status itself fulfilled the ideals of freedom and human dignity, and in 1956 the PDP officially took the line that the commonwealth was not a transitional

status toward independence or statehood but a permanent arrangement. Nevertheless, the debate on status had not ceased. The
shift of the PDP from independentism to a permanent semi-independent position had narrowed the gap between its solution and
that of the Republican statehood party. This factor, combined with
the latter's position on social and economic matters somewhat to the
right of the PDP, may have helped it in gaining more support in
the 1950s. In 1964 the statehood party polled more than a third of the
votes, and by that time the PDP's stand on the permanence of commonwealth status seemed rather less firm and the possibility of it
accepting statehood perhaps somewhat less remote.

The overwhelming reason for the rejection of independence was
economic. Without access to federal funds and the free movement of persons and goods provided by a common citizenship and
a common external tariff, Puerto Rico's economy could not have
developed in the remarkable way it did. As has already been noted,
development made Puerto Rico even more closely dependent economically on the United States and independence, unless accompanied by a continuance of the same economic relationship (which
it seemed the United States Congress could never approve), would
have been fatal. Statehood, the traditional alternative, would, of
course, have guaranteed Puerto Rico's economic security, in
addition to which the island would have been entitled to direct representation in Congress and could still have received federal funds
on a large scale. Moreover, its position would have been that of a
full member of the American family with the full rights of all other
states, rather than that of a poor relation subsisting on America's
charity and favor. On the other hand, statehood would have been
costly, as the valuable privileges of exemption from federal income
tax and the remission to the Puerto Rican treasury of duties col-
lected on Puerto Rican goods sold in the United States would have
been lost. Furthermore, it would have been virtually irrevocable,
and would have been likely to lead to a more complete assimilation into the American way of life. While many Puerto Rican advocates of statehood would have welcomed this, the submergence of
Puerto Rican identity probably would have been resisted by a majority of the islanders. Commonwealth status, however, falling short
of complete integration, gave more hope for the preservation of
Puerto Rico's culture and left the way open for either extreme
solution in the future. At the same time, in spite of the praise lav-

ished on this solution by its creators, the powers it gave the island government were more appropriate to a unit in a federation than to an independent country.

FEDERATION AND INDEPENDENCE

The problem of political advance in the British territories was a complex one. While the aim of the British colonial administration was progress toward "dominion status," which meant autonomy both in internal and external affairs and equality of status with other members of the Commonwealth under the British Crown, it was generally held, up to the end of World War II, that to become independent as a dominion, a colony had to be viable—reasonably large in population and capable of supporting itself financially and economically. In the Caribbean area there were fourteen separate administrative units, most with small populations of under 100,000 and only one with over a million inhabitants. None of these appeared to qualify for independence on its own. On the other hand, aggregated together they might make a nation large enough to be viable as a dominion. The Colonial Office had, in fact, long been interested in some form of closer association of the West Indian territories, mainly for reasons of administrative convenience. But most proposals had met with local resistance, largely because the territories each had more contact with the metropolis than with any of the neighboring colonies, and the Colonial Office decided not to proceed further with any schemes until local opinion was more favorable.

At the end of World War II the auspices seemed more encouraging. Practical cooperation was increasing. The Colonial Office's Development and Welfare Organization for the West Indies, set up during the war with its headquarters in Barbados, was tackling economic and social problems on a regional basis, and organizations such as trade unions and chambers of commerce in individual territories were beginning to cooperate with their opposite numbers in other islands. Regional bodies of this sort, as well as political parties in some places, had begun to express themselves clearly in favor of association at governmental level. In view of the insular separation of the various colonies and the successful precedents of federations of adjacent colonies in Canada and Australia, a federal association was the only form given serious consideration either in Britain or the West Indies. In 1945 the British government requested the governments of the various territories to look into the question of federation. The reaction was generally favorable, and at a conference held in Jamaica in 1947 the island colonies, with the exception of the Bahamas and the Virgin Islands, which were closely bound up economically with the United States and the American Virgin Islands respectively, agreed in principle to form a federation. The mainland territories of British Guiana and British Honduras were less enthusiastic, and, although they continued to participate in subsequent meetings as observers, ultimately declined to join in. With their tracts of empty land, they might perhaps have served to complement the overpopulated islands, and indeed a commission reported favorably on their possibilities for large-scale land settlement in 1948. But many people in both territories were apprehensive of the consequences of immigration, and some also felt that their destiny lay rather toward the interior of the continent than toward the sea and the neighboring islands. With British Guiana and British Honduras opting out of federation, the prospects of creating a West Indian nation on a balanced and viable economic basis were much reduced.

The primary purpose of federation, from the West Indian point of view, was not, however, economic but political. The urgent demand was for self-government and in the late 1940s it appeared that the British government would not concede this to individual islands, but only to a federation. It quickly became clear that federation was to be very much a marriage of convenience between parties that were highly suspicious of each other and not prepared to submerge their particular interests and their individual identities in an integrated nation. The eight smaller territories, Barbados, Antigua, St. Kitts, Montserrat, Dominica, St. Lucia, St. Vincent, and Grenada (whose combined population was less than a quarter of that of the federation) feared that they would be dominated by Jamaica (with over half the population) and Trinidad (which had the remaining quarter). They thus sought to defend themselves by insisting on having a much greater say in the federal government than would have been justified on a strict basis of representation according to population. The larger islands were more concerned with the economic implications, for it was expected that federation in any form would almost necessarily involve the free movement of persons and goods between its constituent parts. For the relatively prosperous Trinidad this meant the likelihood of unrestricted immigration from the small islands and the consequent inheritance of their unemployment problems. For Jamaica a federal customs union would necessitate the reduction of some of the high tariffs which not only formed a significant part of her revenue but which also constituted an important element in the development of her infant industries. In such circumstances negotiations were protracted. Final agreement was not reached until 1956, and then only on what was a federation in little more than name, with an extremely weak central government and the really important questions, such as free movement of persons and goods, accepted only in principle, their implementation being left aside for future consideration.

One issue that could not be shelved indefinitely was that of the location of the federal capital, for when the federal government was set up it would have to convene somewhere. In early discussions the general opinion had been that the capital should be on one of the smaller islands where it would be in a neutral position in relation to the larger territories and where it would be able to give a boost to one of the poorer economies. But as time went on many came to reckon that the expense involved in developing the necessary facilities from the basis of a town of no more than 20,000 inhabitants would be too great a burden on the area, and in 1956 the whole question was thrown open. Almost all the territories asserted their claims and, for the first time, popular interest in federation throughout the West Indies ran high. The report of a committee of outside geographical experts disposed of the arguments for the smaller islands, and narrowed the choice to Barbados, Jamaica, and Trinidad, from which the West Indian delegations finally selected Trinidad. Unfortunately, however, the capital site issue had been one calculated to arouse interisland jealousy and local patriotism, rather than to develop sentiments of common West Indian nationhood, and the inevitable disappointment of all territories but one produced something of an antifederal reaction. This was noticeable particularly in Jamaica, the largest and most isolated of the units. Once the possibility of Jamaica as the head and center of the federation, with a string of dependencies in the eastern Caribbean, no longer existed, many Jamaicans began to have second thoughts about the whole federal idea.

A vital element in Jamaica's reappraisal of federation was the change which took place in the 1950s in the ideas of the British government, and indeed of world opinion, about the necessary criteria for independence. By 1957 it appeared not improbable that the Colonial Office would be prepared to regard Jamaica as eligible for independence on its own. In 1947 federation had seemed the only way to independence; ten years later there was a choice, and Jamaica was inevitably more critical in its view of the federal path. Indeed, for Jamaica, federation had virtually lost its original *raison d'être,* and continued Jamaican participation had to be justified in terms of the positive advantages of a wider nationhood. For many Jamaicans these were offset by financial considerations. Although the Colonial Office made clear that financial aid to the West Indies would not end with independence, it did not state precisely what aid would be forthcoming, and it was fairly obvious that, within an independent federation, the ultimate financial responsibility for the smaller islands, whose budgets were assisted by grants-in-aid from Britain, would have to be shouldered by Jamaica and Trinidad. This point was strongly stressed by the Jamaican opposition party, led by Sir Alexander Bustamante, which in 1957 adopted a marked antifederal line. On the other hand, during the years when federal arrangements were being worked out, the idea of West Indian nationhood based on a common ethnic and cultural heritage had been propagated and the possibilities of regional economic planning and the pooling of numerous common services had been explored. Jamaica had to consider whether such positive benefits were likely to outweigh the additional financial burden that federation seemed likely to involve, and detached appraisal of the pros and cons was not easy after federation became a matter of island party politics.

There were certainly some grounds for scepticism about the possible advantages of federation, for the federal government had been made so weak that it was unlikely to be able to play much of a positive role in regional developments. The potentialities of federal nationhood could only be fully realized if more powers were transferred from the units to the central government. This was, in fact, being advocated by Dr. Eric Williams, Chief Minister of Trinidad (who had only come into power in late 1956 after the form of the federal constitution had been settled), and others had, all along, worked for a greater centralization of power. But in general, the political leaders of the units had shown themselves reluctant to surrender powers to the federal government. Unless the leading politicians became prepared to enter wholeheartedly into the federal experiment and place the nation before the individual island, it was unlikely that the federal government would be given much opportunity to develop.

The attitude of the political leaders to the federation was quickly put to the test, for the federal constitution provided that no person could serve at the same time in the legislature of one of the unit territories and in the parliament of the federation. Thus, before the first federal elections in 1958, the politicians had to decide whether to stand for election to the federal parliament, or stay in local island politics. The immediate attractions of federal politics were limited because of the federation's restricted powers and resources, for, although the federation was destined to proceed to independence, when it was set up it enjoyed no greater degree of self-government in relation to Britain than did some of the units. For many holders of island ministerial posts, moving from unit to federal government would have meant moving to a position of less responsibility and would have signified an act of faith in the future of the federation. It is hardly surprising that many of the leaders throughout the area decided to stay at home. The most critical and probably the most difficult decision was that of Norman Manley, leader of the Jamaican government party, who was aware that if he went to the federal parliament, he would, in all probability, become the first prime minister of the West Indies. But, with the Jamaican opposition antifederal and his own supporters by no means solidly profederal, he had also to consider that the position of his party and of his policies for Jamaican development might well be endangered if he were to leave the island political scene. On the other hand, he had to reckon that, if the leader of the largest and most self-governing unit declined federal office, the federal government, and the emerging nation it was supposed to embody, would almost certainly remain very weak. In deciding to remain at the head of affairs in his island, Manley accorded Jamaica a higher priority than the West Indies, but in doing so he acted no differently from most West Indian politicians in the previous decade, who, in the deliberations over federation, had almost invariably put insular considerations before national.

Manley's example was widely followed. No front-rank Jamaican politician stood for federal election, nor did Williams and his ministerial colleagues in Trinidad. Their followers showed a similar disregard for federal politics. The Federal Labor Party, a coalition of most of the governing parties in the different islands which had expected to win handsomely, gained less than half the seats in Trinidad and less than one third in Jamaica and only obtained a narrow majority in the federal parliament by carrying almost all the small island seats. With small and weak delegations from the major islands, leadership in the Federal Labor Party, when it took office, devolved on the small islanders. Sir Grantley Adams of Barbados became Federal Prime Minister, his deputy was a St. Lucian, and his finance minister from St. Kitts. This did not help to commend the Federal Government to the larger territories, which had all along felt that the eight smaller territories, each with its separate delegation, had been able to wield too great an influence over the setting up of the federation.

Before the end of 1958 Adams had clashed with Manley, by warning the Jamaican government that when the taxing powers of the federation were enlarged these might be used, and indeed used retroactively, to intervene, in the interests of the nation as a whole, in measures that were being taken for Jamaica's economic development. To Jamaicans it seemed that national coordination might well prove harmful rather than beneficial, and there was talk of secession. Manley, however, proceeded to negotiate amendments to the federal constitution which increased Jamaica's parliamentary representation; by 1961 he had secured for his island a virtual veto over any federal measure liable to affect its vital interests and had ascertained that the British government would not oppose Jamaica seeking independence on its own, if the island so chose. Shortly afterward the whole question was submitted to a referendum, in which the Jamaican electorate decided to withdraw from the federation.

It is possible that the Jamaican voters considered that a federation that had been made so weak that it could do Jamaica no harm was not likely to be able to do the island much good either; but local party issues also entered into the referendum, which in part represented a swing away from Manley's party, which lost the island elections in the following year. For a few months there were still hopes that the truncated federation might survive, but early in 1962 the Trinidad government declared that it also would proceed to separate independence as it was not prepared to carry the financial burden of the poorer islands under a federal arrangement, but that any of the islands that wished to join the unitary state of Trinidad and Tobago could negotiate for that purpose. Only Grenada gave serious consideration to this possibility, but nothing came of it. The federal idea persisted among the smaller territories, which for some years negotiated to form a federation of the "Little Eight"; but by 1965 no agreement had been reached, and in the course of 1966 Barbados became independent and the others (with the exception of Montserrat) entered into a new semi-autonomous constitutional arrangement with Britain. The West Indies federation had been formally dissolved in May 1962, with both Jamaica and Trinidad and Tobago becoming independent in August of that year.

Many reasons, from the lack of vision of parochially minded West Indian politicians to the parsimony of the British government, have been suggested for the failure of the federation. There certainly were many contributory factors, but, basically, all the territories found that the only thing they were prepared to make sacrifices for was independence and, once that was no longer indissolubly linked to federation, federal association offered little to compensate for the compromise of sovereignty it demanded. A West Indian federation with a total population of some three million, scattered among islands with similar dependent economies, did not seem likely to be significantly more viable in the modern world than Jamaica, with half that population. The prospects for Trinidad looked better if it were on its own than if it were burdened with eight poor relations. The small islands were not prepared to lose their identity and to throw in their lot with their larger neighbors without special safeguards for their individual interests. Dependent on external financial aid, they were wary of allowing financial responsibility to be transferred from a distant, relatively wealthy, benevolently inclined Britain to a closer, poorer, necessarily more stringent Federal Government. The idea of federation was a product of concepts of criteria for nationality which became outmoded as the twentieth century entered its second half, and national independence was seen to be a relative matter and interdependence an essential feature of international relations.

The various developments since the 1930s have undoubtedly made most of the West Indian territories much less colonial in their social structures, their economies, and their political forms. The area, however, has not yet succeeded in divesting itself entirely of the colonial psychology and dependent mentality rooted in its historical experience. As the West Indies and the Guianas reach the end of the colonial road and struggle to take their places among the modern nations, one can only hope that they have not had their prospects permanently impaired by being colonies too long.

Few historical works cover precisely the same geographical area as the present volume. Much of the history of the area has been written from the point of view of the individual metropolitan empires, and although in recent years the trend has been toward a more regional approach, this has not yet given rise to an extensive bibliography. The best general history of the region is John H. Parry and Philip M. Sherlock, *A Short History of the West Indies* (London, 1956), which deals with Cuba and Hispaniola as well as the territories discussed in this study. A number of other works have used a regional or comparative approach for particular periods and aspects. Arthur P. Newton's *The European Nations in the West Indies, 1493-1688* (London, 1933) is an admirable general survey of the early history of the region, and Sir Harold Mitchell's *Europe in the Caribbean: The Policies of Great Britain, France and the Netherlands towards their West Indian Territories in the Twentieth Century* (Edinburgh, 1963) concentrates on the period since World War II. The British territories in the 1940s are compared with the American in Mary Proudfoot, *Britain and the United States in the Caribbean: A Comparative Study in Methods of Development* (London, 1954), and essays on developments in the whole of the dependent Caribbean in the 1950s are included in A. Curtis Wilgus, ed., *The Caribbean: British, Dutch, French, United States* (Gainesville, Fla., 1958). Richard Pares' *War and Trade in the West Indies, 1739-1763* (Oxford, 1936; reprinted London, 1963) discusses British and French, and to a lesser extent Spanish, possessions and policies, and the same writer's *Merchants and Planters* (Cambridge, 1960) and *Yankees and Creoles: The Trade between North America and the West Indies before the American Revolution* (London, 1956), and the two volumes by the Hon. Hugh A. Wyndham on *The Atlantic and Slavery* (London, 1935) and *The Atlantic and Emancipation* (London, 1937) treat of both British and French islands in wider contexts. Also wider in scope, but of great value for West Indian history, are Elizabeth Donnan, ed., *Documents Illustrative of the History of the Slave Trade to America* (4 vols.,

137

Washington, 1930-35; reprinted New York, 1965) and Noel Deerr, *The History of Sugar* (2 vols., London, 1949-50).

Most historical writing about the West Indies has, however, confined itself at widest to the possessions of a single power. There is a substantial bibliography on the British territories, the earlier phases of which are discussed in some detail in Elsa V. Goveia, *A Study on the Historiography of the British West Indies to the End of the Nineteenth Century* (Mexico, 1956), and the more recent more briefly in David A. G. Waddell, "The British West Indies" in Robin W. Winks, ed., *The Historiography of the British Empire-Commonwealth* (Durham, N.C., 1966), but much less in English on the non-British empires. General histories are few. Sir Alan Burns, *A History of the British West Indies* (London, 1954) contains a substantial body of facts, but seldom rises above the level of compilation. William L. Burn, *The British West Indies* (London, 1951) provides a brief sketch. W. Adolphe Roberts, *The French in the West Indies* (New York, 1942) and Philip H. Hiss, *Netherlands America* (New York, 1943) are popular general surveys.

Much more has been written on shorter periods or specialized topics within the history of individual empires, with the emphasis strongly on the seventeenth and eighteenth centuries when the West Indies were of greatest importance to the European imperial powers. Among the more valuable of such works are Nellis M. Crouse, *French Pioneers in the West Indies, 1624-1664* (New York, 1940) and *The French Struggle for the West Indies, 1665-1713* (New York, 1943); Archibald P. Thornton, *West India Policy under the Restoration* (Oxford, 1956); Stewart L. Mims, *Colbert's West India Policy* (New Haven, Conn., 1912); Frank W. Pitman, *The Development of the British West Indies, 1700-1763* (New Haven, Conn., 1917); Lowell J. Ragatz, *The Fall of the Planter Class in the British Caribbean, 1763-1833* (New York, 1928; reprinted New York, 1963); Eric Williams, *Capitalism and Slavery* (Chapel Hill, N.C., 1944; London, 1964); David J. Murray, *The West Indies and the Development of Colonial Government, 1801-1834* (Oxford, 1965); William L. Burn, *Emancipation and Apprenticeship in the British West Indies* (London, 1937); and Raymond W. Beachey, *The British West Indies Sugar Industry in the Late 19th Century* (Oxford, 1957).

Many works on West Indian history deal with only a single territory. Clinton V. Black, *The Story of Jamaica* (London, 1965); Michael Craton, *A History of the Bahamas* (London, 1962); Gordon C. Merrill, *The Historical Geography of St. Kitts and Nevis, The West Indies* (Mexico, 1958); and Eric Williams, *History of the Peoples of Trinidad and Tobago* (Port-of-Spain, 1962; London, 1964) provide general historical outlines, as do two works which deal mainly with the present: Raymond T. Smith, *British Guiana* (London, 1962) and David A. G.

Waddell, *British Honduras: A Historical and Contemporary Survey* (London, 1961).

Some useful historical material is also to be found in economic, social, and political studies, such as Otis P. Starkey, *The Economic Geography of Barbados* (New York, 1939); Jan H. Adhin, *Development Planning in Surinam in Historical Perspective* (Utrecht, 1961); John Y. and Dorothy L. Keur, *Windward Children: A Study in Human Ecology of the Dutch Windward Islands in the Caribbean* (Assen, 1960); and Gordon K. Lewis, *Puerto Rico: Freedom and Power in the Caribbean* (New York, 1963).

Many of the best contributions to Caribbean history are studies of short periods or particular aspects of the history of an individual territory, such as Elsa V. Goveia, *Slave Society in the British Leeward Islands at the End of the Eighteenth Century* (New Haven, Conn., 1965); George Metcalf, *Royal Government and Political Conflict in Jamaica, 1729-1783* (London, 1965); Philip D. Curtin, *Two Jamaicas: The Role of Ideas in a Tropical Colony, 1830-1865* (Cambridge, Mass., 1955); Douglas G. Hall, *Free Jamaica, 1838-1865: An Economic History* (New Haven, Conn., 1959); Robert A. Humphreys, *The Diplomatic History of British Honduras, 1638-1901* (London, 1961); Dwarka Nath, *A History of Indians in British Guiana* (London, 1950); Waldemar Westergaard, *The Danish West Indies under Company Rule* (New York, 1917); Arturo Morales-Carrión, *Puerto Rico and the Non-Hispanic Caribbean: A Study in the Decline of Spanish Exclusivism* (Rio Piedras, P.R., 1952); Thomas Mathews, *Puerto Rican Politics and the New Deal* (Gainesville, Fla., 1960); and Charles T. Goodsell, *Administration of a Revolution: Executive Reform in Puerto Rico under Governor Tugwell, 1941-1946* (Cambridge, Mass., 1965). Particularly illuminating are three first-rate case studies, J. Harry Bennett's *Bondsmen and Bishops: Slavery and Apprenticeship on the Codrington Plantations of Barbados, 1710-1838* (Berkeley, Calif., 1958); Sidney W. Mintz's, *Worker in the Cane: A Puerto Rican Life History* (New Haven, Conn., 1960); and Richard Pares' outstanding history of a single planter and merchant family over a century and a half, *A West-India Fortune* (London, 1950).

Much valuable material on West Indian history has appeared, and continues to appear, in a great variety of metropolitan learned journals. Two local periodicals *Caribbean Studies*, published quarterly by the Institute of Caribbean Studies of the University of Puerto Rico, and *Social and Economic Studies*, published quarterly by the Institute of Social and Economic Research of the University of the West Indies, print some historical articles, and the *Jamaican Historical Review*, formerly devoted largely to insular antiquarian material, announced in 1965 its intention to widen its scope and publish scholarly articles concerned with the history of any part of the Caribbean area.

There are, as yet, few collections of contemporary materials on West Indian history presented in the form of "readings." *Sources of West Indian History* (London, 1962), compiled by Fitzroy R. Augier and Shirley C. Gordon, is a useful general introductory volume of short selections, mainly relating to British territories. Two more specialized collections of extracts are *A Century of West Indian Education: A Source Book* (London, 1963), compiled with commentary by Shirley C. Gordon, which deals with the larger British colonies since emancipation, and *Documents on British West Indian History, 1807-1833* (Port-of-Spain, 1962), compiled and edited by Eric Williams, who is also the compiler of *Documents of West Indian History*, Vol. 1, 1492-1655 (Port-of-Spain, 1963), the first of five projected volumes of what promises to be a most valuable series.

AREA AND POPULATION OF THE WEST INDIAN TERRITORIES

	Area in Square Miles	Population and Date of Estimate
Independent Nations		
Jamaica	4,411	1,827,000 (1966)
Trinidad and Tobago	1,980	979,000 (1965)
Guyana	83,000	655,000 (1965)
Barbados	166	245,000 (1965)
British Dependencies		
Antigua	171	64,000 (1965)
Bahamas	4,404	138,000 (1965)
British Honduras (Belize)	8,867	109,000 (1966)
Cayman Islands	93	8,000 (1960)
Dominica	305	65,000 (1964)
Grenada	133	94,000 (1964)
Montserrat	32	14,000 (1964)
St. Kitts-Nevis-Anguilla	155	59,000 (1966)
St. Lucia	238	99,000 (1964)
St. Vincent	150	87,000 (1964)
Turks and Caicos Islands	202	6,000 (1964)
Virgin Islands	59	8,000 (1964)
Departments of France		
Guadeloupe	687	297,000 (1963)
Martinique	431	303,000 (1963)
Guyane (French Guiana)	35,135	35,000 (1963)
Parts of the Kingdom of the Netherlands		
Netherlands Antilles	371	206,000 (1966)
Surinam (Dutch Guiana)	54,144	330,000 (1963)
United States Dependencies		
Puerto Rico	3,435	2,573,000 (1964)
Virgin Islands	133	40,000 (1964)

INDEX